ACRYLIC ART IS FUN III

This book is based on the T.V. Series "Acrylic Art is Fun III."
Produced by Graphics Plus of Florida, Inc.

CONTENTS

Publisher: Graphics Plus of Florida, Inc.
Author, Artist and Creator of Instruction Methods: Brenda Harris
Editor: Marcia Meara
Production Director: Florence Daniels
Production Assistant: Barbara J. Bauer/Kelsey R. Cupples
Photographer: Creative Photographic Services, Inc.
Roger Harris

ISBN 0-943295-12-2
Library of Congress Catalog Card Number: 87-83531   First Printing 1990   Printed in USA

Dedication

This book is dedicated to you! Because of all the *fantastic* letters to the publisher, Graphics Plus of Florida, and to television stations all over the U.S., this, my fourth series and book is a reality. I sincerely hope my efforts bring you many hours of enjoyment. **I THANK YOU!**

A word from b.Harris

Art is fun! It puts purpose in your life. We are all born knowing nothing. As with everything we accomplish in life, learning to paint is a step-by-step progression. As you progress, your family, friends, and others will see your talents emerge. They will see you getting better and better as you realize your own self worth. Your most important tool for this is a *positive attitude*.

Realizing that you will have trying times, peaks and valleys, so to speak. I share with you my favorite word - "YET." "Yet is the magic three-letter word that will save you a lot of four-letter words. Never say, "I can't, I haven't, I don't know how" etc., without *"yet"* close behind. Smile and say "I haven't mastered this *yet*" or "I don't do this as well as I would like to, *yet*. Using *"yet"* in this way, helps you develop a positive attitude necessary for improvement and ultimately success.

Learning to paint is easy when you have fun and follow the rules. The rules are study, practice and achieve the realistic goals you set for yourself. GO FOR IT!

Acknowledgements

Many people deserve a word of thanks for helping me assemble ACRYLIC ART IS FUN III, both the book and the television series. I could not have accomplished this alone. THANK YOU!

To my friend, Marcia Meara, for unselfishly volunteering your time, knowledge, and skills. You helped me organize my thoughts, type and proof read. When I needed it most, your quick wit made me laugh and kept me lighthearted when the pressure was on. You are one in a million! I treasure your friendship. I could not have done it without you!

To my WXEL friends: Your professional team work transforms an ordinary days work into a fun, creative, production. Jim Moran, thanks for your encouragement. Celeste, thanks for being a patient director. As for the crew, you're the greatest! Thanks for "Mr. Bunz."

To my students: Your enthusiasm and desire to learn and paint more has inspired me. It was you who supplied most of the ideas for this and my other books. I could not have accomplished this without your confidence and support. I treasure every one of you and wish you the very best.

To the art and craft store owners who have invited me into their shops, homes and hearts over the past years... a very special thanks. You have made me feel "at home." It seems we have been friends forever!

To my computer programmer, teacher, and friend, John Gibson, for willingly coming to my studio day after day, week after week, to install software, program the computer, and teach Roger and I how to operate it. Without your expertise and patience, I would still be on "page one." I value you as a true friend and could not have done it without you. Thanks!

A special thanks to the sponsors of my TV series. I consider it an honor to be associated with such fine organizations as Graphics Plus of Florida, Inc., Langnickel Artist Brushes, Inc., Dalee Book Company, and Saral Paper Co., Inc. Thank you for your confidence in me.

To my husband: Roger, not only have you taken care of all the cooking and cleaning, but you have been my "right hand," assisting me every step of the way. This book does not have enough pages to list all the reasons why I appreciate you. Thanks for being a "sport" and standing by me. I love you!

To Jeff, Alfie, and Jasmine: You put a spark in my life that provides me unmeasurable joy. You have my undying love and affection. Thanks for being super!

An apple for the teacher
      seems quite apropos,
Cause Brenda's quite a teacher
      as we surely know.

To teach our group of learners
      patience it does take,
But to Brenda Harris
      it's just a "piece of cake."

I, for one, am awe-struck
      the way this gal can paint,
Reconstruction all our works
      she has the patience of a saint.

Brenda has a quality
      that's found in very few,
Not only can she paint a scene
      she can teach it too.

Of your classes, Brenda
      we will never tire,
You've that special where-with-all
      that each of us admire.

by Richard (Dick) Morse

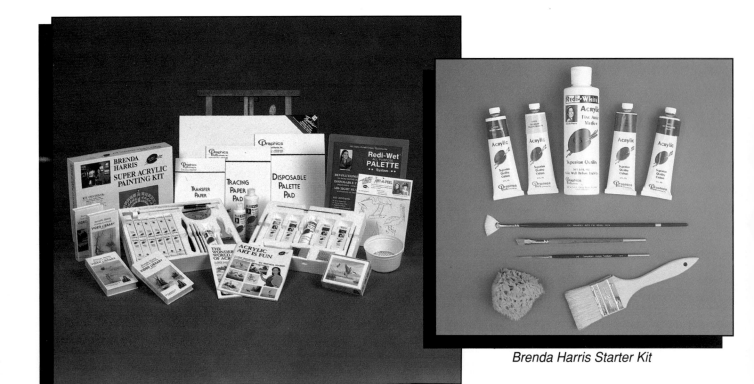

Supplies

Brenda Harris Starter Kit

TOOLS OF THE TRADE

Execution of the techniques in this series is dependent upon the quality and selection of products used. The following are recommended:

Graphics Plus of Florida, Inc. ACRYLIC PAINTS

All acrylics are not created equal! Density, viscosity and colors often vary from brand to brand. For the techniques illustrated in this book, your acrylics should be moist and creamy in order to blend together nicely, yet have a high proportion of pigment in them. GPF paints and Redi-White© are specially designed to create the results shown here. Be sure to look for my picture and the Graphics Plus of Florida logo to identify clearly these products in your art supply store.

In addition to Redi-White©, Redi-Gel©, and Redi-Mask©, the paints used in this book are:

Ultramarine Blue (UB)   Chrome Oxide Green (COG)
Burnt Umber (BU)   Yellow Ochre (= yellow oxide = YO)
Burnt Sienna (BS)   Indo Orange Red (IOR)
Hookers Green (HG)   Permanent Green Light (PGL)
Phthalo Green (PG)   Cadmium Red Medium (CRM)
Acra Violet (AV)   Cadmium Yellow Medium (CYM)
Cadmium Orange (CO)

Redi-Gel©

This heavy bodied paint dries clear and glossy. For this book, I mixed it with water and GPF acrylic colors to produce both heavy bodied, and exquisitly transparent glazes, it also lengthens working time.

Redi-Mask©

This masking solution works as a protective coating to prevent paint from adhering to a particular area.

Graphics Plus of Florida, Inc. REDI-WHITE©

Redi-White© by GPF is unlike any other acrylic paint on the market. This liquid white paint is specially mixed for proper consistency and opaque qualities to afford soft, subtle colors and coverage every time. By delaying the drying process, Redi-White© allows even the beginner to achieve beautiful blends of colors.

Not only is Redi-White© a *must* when mixing and blending soft colors, it is benchmark for determining proper paint consistency. With few exceptions, your paint should be the same creamy, fluid consistency as Redi-White©; therefore, dark colors generally require the addition of more water than light colors, as they have little or no Redi-White©.

I cannot over-emphasize the importance of Redi-White®. You must have it! There is no substitute!

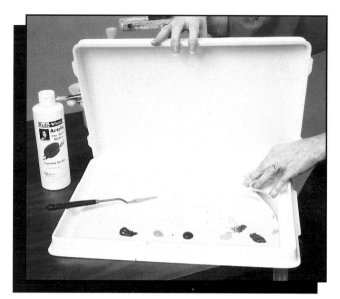

Redi-Wet Palette System®

REDI-WET PALETTE SYSTEM®

The new Redi-Wet Palette System® introduced in this series will keep your paints wet for weeks!

The system consists of a palette, sponge and special acrylic palette film.

Soak the thin sponge and the special acrylic film in water until both are saturated, preferably overnight. Place the saturated sponge on the palette and add sufficient water to the sponge to keep it soggy. Place the special film on top of the sponge. Moisture from the sponge comes through the special film at a controlled pace, keeping the GPF paints and Redi-White® wet. By placing and securing the lid on your palette system, you can return to your paints days or weeks later and enjoy the same creamy consistency.

Should your special film develop dry areas when uncovered, lift the film, add clean, cold water to the sponge in that area, then press down on the film. This will restore the lost moisture.

Langnickel

A R T I S T S '   B R U S H E S

QUALITY of brushes will vary with each manufacturer. This is where experience tells me that Langnickel Select Artist Brushes are superior.

I use and recommend Langnickel brushes. Not only are they the finest quality, they are also an excellent value!

It is essential that you acquire the proper assortment of brushes in order to execute the variety of techniques you are going to learn from this text and my television series.

You will need a variety of sizes, shapes and bristle content. I recommend that you start with and stick to this original set. Later you may wish to expand your assortment.

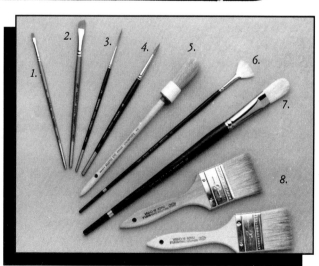

1. Flat Combo, 2. Angular Brush, 3. Liner Brush, 4. Round Brush, 5. Foliage Stippling Brush, 6. Fan Brush, 7. Large Filbert Bristle Brush, 8. Blending Brushes

Background Brush
(2" Blending Brush)

These two-inch-wide brushes are made from quality Chinese bristles. They are designed to blend colors on the canvas as smooth as silk, establish large areas of grass or, if you choose, successfully stipple-in distant foliage.

Everyone needs two background brushes — one for dark colors in the sky, water or grass, and one for light areas. I prefer working with three — the third kept clean (free of paint) and towel dried for blending only. Extra brushes eliminate a lot of rinsing. I also use and enjoy the 1/2" and 1" sizes.

Angular Brush (3/8")

Because of its shape and bristle content, this brush offers the acrylic artist the best of all worlds!

It offers the performance of a flat brush, holding sharp edges without splitting, yet its unique shape enables you to build boats, barns and houses as if you were a seasoned carpenter. Its unique blend of natural and man-made fibers offers the softness of the finest sables and the remarkable snap and resilience unique to synthetic fibers.

Liner Brush (Size 2)

This tiny little brush transforms an ordinary painting into a masterpiece! Made with a combination of longer fibers to hold lots of color, this full-bodied brush maintains a needle sharp, split-proof point.

Round Brush (Size 6)

Because of the unique blend of man-made and natural fibers, this brush maintains a perfect point, yet possesses an amazing spring that is vital to the sharp focused detail, lovely washes, and shadowing techniques I teach. Add larger and smaller sizes later. For acrylics, I prefer this brush to a sable.

Fan Brush (Size 2)

I cannot over-emphasize the importance of selecting the right fan brush. Its shape makes all fan brushes appear the same to a beginner, which could not be further from the truth. This finest quality, hog hair fan brush is more versatile than any other brush. I use it to make tree trunks, foliage, grass, roads, clouds, water, waves and even for blending. It is good for almost everything! You may even discover a special use that I don't cover in this series. You cannot get the sharp focus, controlled look of my paintings with a lesser quality brush. Having extra fan brushes saves time and paint, eliminating frequent rinsing to change colors. The size 2 is the most versatile.

Foliage Stippling Brush

This uniquely shaped round Chinese bristle brush is not only used for creating and highlighting foliage, it is great for blustery skies and backgrounds and is an excellent blender! I use both the size 2 and 4.

Large Filbert Bristle Brush (Size 8)
(Cloud Blending Brush)

This finest quality, pure hog hair bristle filbert is soft, pliable and sturdy. Its shape makes blending clouds a snap! Use it for small blending jobs and large tree trunks.

ADDITIONAL NECESSARY TOOLS

Palette Knife (P-4)

Because of its flexible blade and angled handle, I use a Langnickel p-4 palette knife for mixing paints, and also as a painting tool for rocks, mountains, tree bark, barn boards, etc.

Natural Sponge

A hand-sized "lacy" natural sponge is a must. Not only is it an amazing tool for painting, but it is also great for wiping off mistakes! You will have fun creating foliage and water splashes with your sponge. It creates amazing results!

Water, Container and Brush Screen

You will need a large container of clean, cold, tap water to mix your paints and to keep your brushes rinsed while painting. A professional brush basin is my favorite; however, a coffee can (or similar size container) with a GPF brush screen is sufficient.

Ruler — clear, plastic 12" T-square

Artist Canvas (Fredrix Red Lable)

Kneaded Eraser

Cotton Terry Towel

Plastic Containers

Blow Dryer

Masking Tape

Toothbrush

Practice Canvas

Watercolor Paper (140 lb. cold pressed)

The canvas covered products in this text provide you a fun and creative way to decorate your home or share your artistic talents with others. Personalized gifts are a treasure!

You will find all the CREATIONS IN CANVAS to be an excellent surface for the acrylic compositions and techniques demonstrated in my books. Preserve your completed project with a clear acrylic sealer. I chose to illustrate a desk set, waste paper basket and tissue holder, and a photograph album. Whatever your choice, I'm sure you will enjoy... CREATIONS IN CANVAS!

TRANSFERRING YOUR PATTERN

For proper results, each artist will need both light and dark wax-free, oil-free transfer paper. Saral is the only manufacturer that I am aware of, that produces this quality of transfer paper. Avoid brands that use an oil or wax base to secure the transferring particles to the paper as they prevent acrylics from adhering properly over the traced lines. I use the white to transfer objects in a dark area and charcoal to transfer over a light area.

Make tracing paper patterns of the black-and-white sketches (opposite the full-page color pictures) in the book. Never put your pattern or transfer paper over wet paint. Properly position the pattern on your dry surface and secure it in place with tape. Slide a piece of Saral transfer paper behind the pattern, and trace the lines onto your surface with a stylus, pen or pencil.

Should you create unwanted smears or have excess lines showing after you have painted the object, dry thoroughly and rub the area briskly with a kneaded eraser. It will not affect the paint, but will remove the transfer.

7

TECHNIQUES

Throughout this book you will notice there are several different methods for creating trees, foliage, skies, water and even birds. I find that giving students a variety of techniques broadens their ability to be independently creative and adventuresome. Mix and mingle these techniques in your compositions.

MIXING YOUR PAINTS

The most common problem that my students incur is not putting enough water in their paint. Remember, keep plenty of cold water handy and add water to your paint mixtures until they are the same fluid consistency as Redi-White®.

Always wet your brush and squeeze out the excess before you go to your paints.

Keep in mind, as you mix your paints, that the basic consistency should compare to that of Red-White®. Should it need to be thicker or thinner I will point this out as we go along. Pre-mix your colors. Scrape the excess off onto your wet palette, for use as needed (Figure 1).

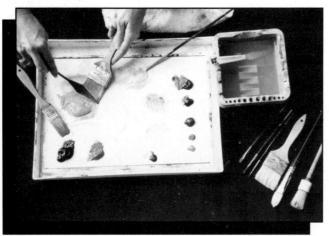
Figure 1

All of us have spread mayonnaise and peanut butter on bread. Use this as your example. Your brush should glide smoothly as if spreading mayonnaise on fresh bread—not like peanut butter. Should your brush begin to stick, skip or drag, add water a little at a time, keeping in mind that it is easier to add than to subtract. I recommend that you touch only one corner of your brush in the water until a circle forms, return to your mixture, and test again. Repeat as necessary. You will learn quickly when it's just right, from your brush mixing on the palette.

There are times when your paint should be thinner or thicker than Redi-White®. These exceptions will be pointed out in the text.

ENLARGING A SKETCH OR PHOTOGRAPH

Draw a light graph across your sketch or photo, then do the same on your tracing paper or canvas. Mark a vertical and a horizontal line to divide the object into four equal quarters. Make two more equidistant horizontal and vertical lines to divide each quarter into quarters. Once your graph is drawn, transfer the photo or drawing line by line, square by square, comparing as you proceed, to make your enlargement or reduction. (I tape my tracing paper to my canvas and grid my tracing paper to avoid erasing unnecessarily on my canvas, then I slip graphite behind my sketch and transfer only the necessary lines.

Another easy way to enlarge or decrease your design or photograph, is to use a copy machine.

MASKING OUT AREAS

Art-A-Peel

These pre-printed patterns designed to correspond with my books make masking out an object a snap. All you do is cut out the peel-and-stick pattern and place it over your sketch. Relax and paint freely over and around it without worry, as it will be "peeled away" when you are ready, leaving the underneath unpainted for your convenience.

Pre printed Art-A-Peel pattern packages are available for ACRYLIC ART IS FUN, books 1, 2 and 3. Blank Art-A-Peel packages are also available to enable you to create your own designs.

Redi-Mask

Apply the Redi-Mask over the areas on your dry surface that you wish to remain paint free. Use an old brush if possible and keep it rinsed frequently. Wash the brush promptly when you have completed your masking with soap and water. Should the Redi-Mask dry in your brush, you will need to clean it with lighter fluid or benzine (turpentine). Certain types of masking liquids will stain, will not protect as intended, and are not water soluble.

Dry the Redi-Mask before you begin painting. Paint freely. Dry again. Remove the masking with an eraser or by simply rubbing it. Presto! No paint underneath.

FAMILIARIZE

Study the color placements in the sky, water, etc. Read through your instructions, visualizing how you are going to execute each step. Have a practice surface handy, (canvas or scrap of watercolor paper, which ever is applicable) to test your colors and strokes before applying them to your painting. This often relieves apprehension.

CORRECTIONS

Sooner or later you will make a boo-boo. We all make mistakes. Relax, they can all be corrected.

If the error is still wet, wipe it off with a clean moist sponge and reapply after the thoroughly cleaned area is once again dry.

If your mistake is dry, you can simply paint over it or scrub it off. To scrub an area off, first moisten it with clean water. Agitate the area with a wet toothbrush. If the dry paint seems stubborn, dunk the toothbrush in Redi-White® and scrub the error as if you were using Ajax. Do not allow the Redi-White® to dry in one area while you scrub in another. Wipe it away and repeat if necessary. It will begin to loosen quickly using this technique.

For super fast elimination of dried paint, use a small metal bristle hardware store brush. Reapply your paint when dry.

Keep in mind that two coats of paint appear darker than one. Try adding a touch of Redi-White® to your same color when patching to eliminate this. Also, when patching an area, fade or wash out the outer edges of the patch with a clean wet brush. This leaves a gradual, barely visible transition.

Once you get the "hang of it," patching is a "Piece of Cake!" You'll be surprised at the results.

SKIES AND BACKGROUNDS

In this text, the sky or background area is applied first. Always mix a sufficient quantity of your sky colors to be used prior to applying anything to your dry canvas. If your first color begins to dry on the canvas before you apply the second, it is very difficult to blend.

Work quickly, blocking in your sky colors with a generous amount of paint. **Overlap** your colors about 1/4" or more, keeping each area nice and clean. Blend softly, moving from light color over darker color (blue gray), with a clean, towel-dried, bristle brush, until the desired effect is achieved.

Do not overwork! Students tend to overwork — stirring until slick spots begin to appear.

Half-dry skies always look streaked. You will have the urge to go back and retouch *right here and there*. **Don't**. Allow it to dry completely. Use a dryer for speed. Visualize your subject matter around your sky, because after your painting is complete, you will find that a streak or two in the sky is very satisfying. If you absolutely cannot accept your sky, do it again after it is completely dry. Sometimes two coats of paint gives it the master's touch.

SMOOTH COLOR TRANSITIONS (Wet-On-Wet)

Generously and quickly cover the entire area with Redi-White® (or appropriate color). *Swish* the premixed colors quickly over this wet paint. Blend with a clean towel-dried brush. Towel clean your brush frequently while blending. (Figure 2)

For streaks of color zipping through the sky, apply and blend with long, even pressure strokes, often going from one side of the canvas to the other.

For a more gradual transition blend with an elongated figure 8 stroke where the colors emerge from the Redi-White®. Apply more pressure on the brush during the initial blending strokes. Lighten up until your brush barely touches the canvas for the final strokes.

This technique is particularly useful for vignettes, where you have a border of color gradually emerging from the edges, or the sky or background color fading into white at the edges. If the composition is divided into sky and water or land, apply the Redi-White® and work only one section at a time.

Figure 2

Smooth Color Transitions (Dry Canvas)

To make a gradual color transition from one color to another, apply the colors quickly and generously to the dry canvas, making sure to overlap the connecting edges of the colors at least 1/4 inch. Quickly, straddle a clean towel-dried brush over the connecting colors and blend using a figure 8 stroke. Towel clean your brush frequently to prevent a muddy appearance. The final blending strokes should be as light as a feather. (Figure 3)

Figure 3

WET-ON-WET CLOUDS

On your dry canvas apply a blue gray or appropriate sky color in an irregular cloud-like shape (Figure 4). Using a different background brush, quickly overlap the bottom edge of the blue gray with Redi-White® or appropriate cloud color. Using small, circular, continuous strokes, push the Redi-White® up from the bottom and about 1/4 inch over the blue gray (Figure 5). Blend and shape the edges with a clean, towel-dried filbert or fan brush. To create a rolling, rounded look, touch just short of the top edge of the cloud, then pull in a semi-circular motion about the size of a small lima bean (Figure 6). Continue this process until the entire top section of the sky is painted.

Cut across the white with the blue gray or one of your accent colors to pull some smaller clouds forward. Add more white and blend with a clean brush (Figure 7). Randomly add and blend in accent colors to act as a back drop for smaller white clouds, creating clouds in front of clouds, inside of the large overall cloud formation. Repeat as often as you like. Leave no distinguishable bottom edges on the clouds. Fill in the remainder of the sky, to the horizon, with Redi-White®. Blend in the accent colors you've chosen to use. I prefer to use long, smooth horizontal strokes of color at the horizon and a more blustery action where the bottom section meets the billowing clouds.

To add more depth to your sky, always have the clouds larger in the top section of the sky and smaller as they move toward the horizon.

Figure 4

Figure 5

Figure 6

Figure 7

10

WET-ON-DRY CLOUDS

Generally, the background colors for this type sky are added quickly and blended wet-into-wet with a towel-dried brush. After the basic sky colors are thoroughly dry, highlight the clouds, one little puff at a time. With your fan brush, apply and leave lots of little bumps and irregularities of your highlight color on the top of each cloud. Fade or scumble out the bottom and inside of the highlight with a clean, very moist bristle filbert brush. Rinse your filbert brush often to keep moist and paint free (Figure 8).

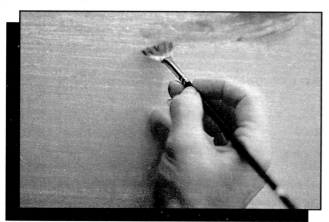

Figure 8

BLUSTERY SKIES/BACKGROUNDS

Blustery skies and backgrounds are fun to paint! Before you begin, familiarize yourself with the finished project for any unique color placement, or a concentration of color in any area. Rub the Redi-White® (Redi-White® with a tint of color) briskly into the pores of the canvas with your blending brush. With your fan brush, randomly tap splotches of your desired colors around in the wet paint (Figure 9). Quickly blend with a foliage stippling brush. Use short, erratic, uneven and circular strokes (Figure 10). Work quickly as this should be accomplished wet-on-wet. You can work one section at a time or all at once.

After this is dry, should you desire, you can change the look with wet-on-dry clouds.

Figure 9

Figure 10

MOUNTAIN AND PALETTE KNIFE ROCKS

Apply base color in the desired shape. With a palette knife, lightly streak your desired colors over the wet base color.

To load your knife properly, spread your color out very thinly on your palette like glaze on a donut. Hold your knife at an angle and scrape up only about 1/8 to 1/4 inch of the spread-out paint onto your knife. You should have a thin thread on the edge. With the knife at a 45-degree angle to the canvas, apply the paint with one quick stroke (Figure 11). Reload often. Clean your knife between colors.

Figure 11

DOUBLE LOADING

This technique allows you to paint two colors at once. It creates an effect that cannot be duplicated by applying the colors separately.

Load your brush with the darkest color of your subject matter; then pull *one side* of your brush through the highlight color creating a dark side and a light side. Turn your brush so that your brush stroke will be half dark and half light as you touch your canvas. I use my liner brush extensively for distant birds, twigs and trees and limbs. For rocks and pebbles, fenceposts, pilings and medium size trees, I use my small #6 round or angle brush.

FOLIAGE

Foliage Stippling Brush
Round Bristle

Many times, especially for oak tree foliage or a more controlled foliage look, I will use my foliage stippling brush to apply the paint. Mix your color and load your brush in one step by holding the brush perpendicular to your palette and pressing up and down into your colors. This will cause the brush to flare out. By lightly tapping your canvas with the flared edges, you can create a lovely leafy look. Highlight colors are loaded into the brush the same way as above, but applied with a lighter touch.

Sponge Technique

A fast and fun way to create foliage is with the sponge. You can tap the paint on with the sponge as shown in my other books, or apply the paint with another tool and tap out the leafy edges and create texture with the sponge.

Fan Brush Stippling
Northern Pines/Fir/Spruce

Load your fan brush by tapping up and down in thick paint. Hold your fan brush vertically and tap the tip top of the tree in. (Figure 12A) Turn the brush horizontally, and add short little branches at the top of the tree. Make them wider as they progress downward (Figure 12B) on the canvas, until the center bristles bend. Push, with an upward thrust, causing the branch tips to curl upward. Zig-zag, back and forth, with these strokes, so as not to make a perfectly cone-shaped tree. (Figure 12C)

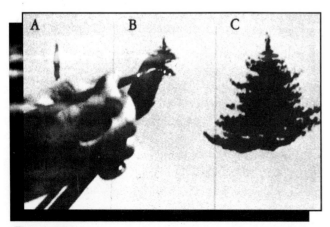

Figure 12

Watercolor Technique

There are times when I use only water to create texture and highlights in the foliage — as in the background trees in "Curing Time."

First fill in the thickest portion of the foliage with paint thinned to the same texture as our Redi-White®. Create an irregular shape (Figure 13). With a clean, damp brush or sponge, tap and pull out tree and bush shapes, creating many shades of colors. Pull color from the outer edges — leave your center dark (Figure 14). Almost any sponge or brush will work; however, the fan and angular brushes and the sponge are my favorites.

Figure 13

Figure 14

HIGHLIGHTING

To create a rounded effect you must have a gradual transition in color on the object (lighthouse, arm, leg, tree, post, etc.) ranging from light to medium to dark.

STIPPLING FOLIAGE HIGHLIGHTS

To achieve a rounded effect when highlighting foliage, tap *lightly*, using less of, and a lighter touch with each additional highlight. Never block out all the base foliage color. Sparingly stipple:

(A)
darkest or dullest highlight about 3/4 way around foliage

(B)
middle value highlight about 1/2 way around

(C)
third or lightest, brightest highlight only on front 1/4

Figure 15

SAND, GRAVEL AND SNOW

Create snow, sand or gravel by loading an old toothbrush with very moist paint. My best results come from holding the brush at a forward angle to the canvas and stroking it with my thumbnail. Often I use more than one color from my painting for contrast (see Figure 16). For small areas or extra control, use your fan brush and flip it with your fingernail or your palette knife. Prevent specks from splattering in inappropriate areas, by shielding with your hand, paper towel, etc.

WASH TECHNIQUES

Transparent Washes (Wet over Dry)

Absolutely beautiful effects are created by this technique that nothing can match. Its uses are boundless. An entire painting can be created with this technique. I particularly like to use it on birds, buildings and boats.

For example, see the tin roof in Figure 17. With the underneath paint dry, pile up a good amount of juicy, rich burnt sienna (Figure 17A); "Wash" or pull color from the bottom edge of your pile of paint, using a clean, wet brush (the angular brush works great here). Let gravity feed the color movement. Pull the color in the direction that the tin will lie, according to the angle of the roof. Notice how the color gradually fades away, yet retains its richness. The white of the canvas "glows" through the transparent wash. You may need to rinse your washing-out brush occasionally, so that you can completely lose the color at the bottom edge (Figure 17B). Try drying this and repeating. You will find two thin washes to be more beautiful than one heavy one. After the roof area is dry, add tin lines and detail using your liner brush (Figure 17C).

When doing these washes, lay only a small area of juicy paint to be washed out, as the outer edge will begin to dry almost immediately. Should you do too large an area, parts may dry before you get to pull the color out. Two brushes work best here: one to lay the color in, and one to fade or wash out.

Remember, for the wash to remain transparent, the underneath color must be dry before you begin. Otherwise, you will get a blend of colors, rather than a glow showing through the wash.

Figure 16

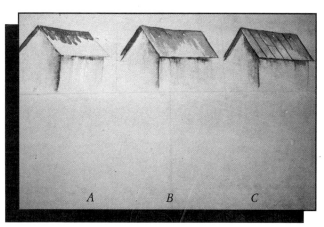

Figure 17

OCEAN/WAVES/WET SAND

When working **wet-on-wet**, apply your chosen colors for the water at the horizon line and down about an inch. Randomly apply the illusion of distant whitecaps with Redi-White® on you liner brush or palette knife. "Tickle" the bottom of the Redi-White® with a *towel-dried* round brush to push up ripples for the top of the wave, and to blend the bottom edge of the Redi-White® into the wet water color. Apply more color as you move forward and make the whitecaps larger and more pronounced. I usually add darker streaks of color in this area and stipple the larger whitecaps just above the darker areas with the fan brush. With a clean, *towel-dried* fan brush swish out the bottom of the Redi-White® with an elongated "C'" stroke (⊂__). Make only one quick stroke per each section the width of the brush on the wave. End each stroke with a long horizontal swish to make the water lay flat again. Stagger a few *"rocking chair"* strokes between the whitecaps with a clean *towel-dried* fan brush to hook the waves together occasionally (∽∽∽). Hook the water and sand colors together with streaks of white and brush horizontally. (see photo P. 60)

To apply the whitecaps **wet-on-dry**, begin by painting the underneath water color as above without the whitecaps and dry (Figure 18, A, B, C). Apply the whitecaps one at a time in the same manner as above, but fade out the bottom edges with a *wet* brush using the same strokes (Figure 18 D, E, F). You can enhance the colors and dry time of your waves by using Redi-Gel as described on page 22, step 2.

Achieve the look of receding water and wet sand by applying streaks of Redi-White® through the dried area where the water and sand colors blend. Apply only a section of a "wash in" at a time and immediately fade or wash out the top edge of this Redi-White® with a clean *wet* brush. Dampening your "wash out" brush with Redi-Gel and water will give you a glossy wet look and extend the drying time.

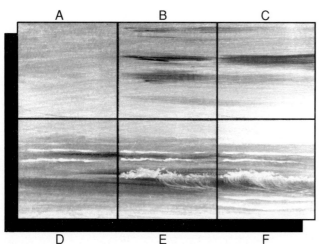

Figure 18

14

Figure 19

WATER AND REFLECTIONS

Water works like a mirror, picking up images and colors around it. In creating a harmonious and realistic effect, I first repeat (reflect) the sky colors in the water. As I add subject matter, I add their reflections in the appropiate color, size and shape. The more movement in the water, the less defined the reflection will be. For this I usually use a zig-zag movement in the reflection.

Don't confuse reflection with shadows. Remember reflection always come toward you (straight down), and shadows always run opposite the light source. Thus, a tree could cast a reflection on the water, toward the viewer and the bottom of the canvas (straight down), and a shadow along the bank in a different direction.

If you visualize your subject matter sitting on a mirror, and paint in the reflection accordingly, making adjustments for movement distortions in the water, you can't go wrong.

Reflections can be done wet-on-wet, or added to a dry painting. When adding a reflection to a dry area, use more water to give it a muted look. Interesting effects can be achieved, as in "Palm Hammock" by wetting the thoroughly dry reflection area with clean water before applying the reflection color. Lightly zig one direction with your fan brush, then zag the other to add shimmer and movement. (See Figure 19)

After the reflection is dry, add very thin horizontal waterlines with very moist Redi-White® or appropriate color. Apply only a couple of waterlines at a time with your liner brush or palette knife to allow you plenty of time to soften some of them (especially their ends) with your finger or a damp brush. This creates a shimmering effect. A clear plastic T-square ruler is handy here, as all the shimmer strokes **must** be perfectly horizontal and parallel to the bottom of the canvas. Never allow them to slope or curl up or down at the ends.

GRASS

Keep this statement in mind as you paint grass: "Grass grows on your canvas just as it does in real life — from the ground up, and with a lot of water."

For thin, wispy grass, I prefer to use my fan brush and very moist paint (more liquid than Redi-White®). Touch a few bristles of the fan brush to your canvas and stroke upward. The pressure should be slightly heavier at the root than the blade tips. Lift up taller grasses with your liner brush (Figure 20).

Figure 20

MARSH GRASSES

Maximum control when painting marsh grasses can be achieved with your fan brush. Alternating and overlapping lights and darks will create a variety of shades. For a deep marsh begin with light values, lengthen your strokes and deepen your shades as you progress forward. Keep your rows of marsh grass flat (parallel to the bottom of the canvas). End with a dark row at the waters edge and reflect the grass by pulling the dark down. Horizontal waterlines are added preferably after the grass color is dry. Apply only a couple of waterlines at a time so as to soften them immediately with a clean damp brush or with your finger to give a shimmering effect (see Figure 21).

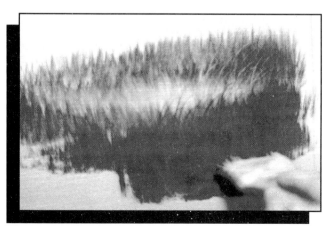

Figure 21

MEADOW GRASSES

For a thick field of grass I often use my large background brushes. With one brush loaded with a light color and the other loaded with dark, work wet-on-wet, alternating your colors. Your paint should be the same consistency as Redi-White®. Holding the brush perpendicular to the canvas, press firmly until the bristles begin to flare out. Hold the pressure firmly and crunch with a slightly upward thrust. Do not allow the bristles to slide upward as it will create a smudge rather than creating the effect of individual grass blades. Done properly, the brush bristles will arch slightly and the top outer bristles will flare out, creating many irregular lengths of grass blades. Use one background brush for the light colors and the other for the dark colors. Use several colors and shades of colors from your composition. Alternate colors and shades of colors in both the light and dark areas. To avoid bare spots, each additional row should be applied, and flare up slightly over the base of the previous one. Generally speaking, to create depth, begin with a light color (in the distance) and end with a dark color (in the foreground at the bottom or your canvas). Adding a contrasting patch of color in an area creates additional depth. (Figure 22)

Figure 22

GRASS POINTERS TO REMEMBER:
1. Brush your strokes from the root up.
2. Use light pressure and lots of water for thin wispy grass.
3. Heavy pressure for thick marsh or field grass, overlapping to avoid bare spots.
4. Use very thin paint and your liner brush for tall grasses and detail.

MORE TECHNIQUES
To learn more fun and interesting techniques join a BRENDA HARRIS ACRYLIC PAINTING WORKSHOP. For more information send a self addressed, stamped envelope.

BRENDA HARRIS WORKSHOPS
P.O. Box 8761
Jacksonville, FL 32239

VIDEO LIBRARY

For more of the techniques used by Brenda Harris, be sure to order her all-new video library series. These one hour, detailed, in-depth programs are designed to show you the many and varied techniques you can use in creating your own works of art.

"WEEKEND RETREAT"
#3231
Vignette Of A Beautiful
Autumn Lake Scene

"GILLIANDS BRIDGE"
#3233
Reminiscent Covered Bridge

"THE GUARDIAN"
#3235
Nesting Mallards In
Their Natural Habitat

"LITTLE TREASURES"
#3237
Little Girl Playing With
Shells On The Beach

TIPS FOR A PROFESSIONAL PAINTING

Contrast
Place your darks against your lights and vice versa.

Scale
Use a variety of shapes and sizes to create interest.

Depth
Three Dimensional Effect
Make objects in the distance higher on the canvas, and less vivid in color and detail. The closer the object is, the larger, more detailed, and lower on the canvas it should be. Overlap distant objects with closer objects in your compositions.

The opposite to this generalization is true for the sky, ie... place large clouds to the top of the sky and make them smaller as you move down toward the horizon.

Corrections
The only people not making mistakes are those unfortunate people who are doing nothing at all. Mistakes are only a *learning experience*. Greet them that way and you will accelerate your learning process fourfold! Anything that you put on your canvas can be corrected. (see CORRECTIONS p.11)

Protect Your Painting
Enhance the colors and protect your art work by spraying your completed, dry canvas with a clear acrylic sealer. Hold the can 10 to 12 inches from your canvas. With a side-to-side motion, spray from top to bottom and back. Turn sideways and repeat, cross-hatching the layers. Select a quality brand.

THE PAINTINGS

Before you begin painting, carefully study each illustrated step.
"A picture is worth a thousand words!"

"FREE LUNCH"
Who says there's no free lunch? Have you
visited the beach lately? Notice how the sea
gulls invite themselves to your food and
never leave so much as a tip, yet no one
ever seems to mind!
To paint this picnic you will need:

Ultramarine Blue (UB)
Cadmium Red Medium (CRM)
Cadmium Yellow Medium (CYM)
Redi-White (RW)
Ultramarine Blue (UB)
Cadmium Red Medium (CRM)
Cadmium Yellow Medium (CYM)
Redi-White (RW)

(Pattern is actual size for 16x20 canvas)

19

STEP: 1

Med. Blue = UB + BU + Redi-White
Teal Blue = UB + PG + Redi-White
Pink = UB + CRM + Redi-White
Phthalo Blue = UB + PG
Tan = BU + Redi-White
Dark Green = BU + PG
Violet Gray = UB + BU + AV + Redi-White

The horizon line is 5" down from the top of a 16" x 20" canvas. The foremost water line is approximately 7 1/2" up from the bottom on the right, and 6" up from the bottom on the left. Position and transfer the little girl so that the bread in her hand is 10 1/4" down from the top and 10 1/4" over from the right of the canvas. Apply your Art-A-Peel.

Cover the sky area with Redi-White using your 2" blending brush. Immediately streak in the pink above the horizon line, the teal in the center, and the medium blue at the top and at random through the sky. Blend with a clean, towel-dried brush. Dry and apply a piece of masking tape just above the water line.

The water and sand are a combination of the colors above with the exception of the dark green. Work quickly applying the water and sand colors so that they blend together without a break. Refer to the photo for color placement. The water should be light at the horizon, darker in the middle, and fade away into the sand at the bottom. Begin with Redi-White + teal at the horizon. Alternate colors and Redi-White as you move forward. The darker streaks are created with phthalo blue. Create sandy areas with tan. Indicate shallow puddles at the edge of the water with lightened blue and teal. Add some darker shadows in the sand with BU and some of your other colors.

Use your fan brush to make the dark green grass short and sparse in the distance, and heavier and darker in the foreground. Dry.

STEP: 2

Use very watery paint, and your fan brush or tooth-brush to speckle the sand with BU, Redi-White, CYM + RW, and your sky colors.

Prepare your washing medium by mixing approximately equal parts Redi-Gel and water in a disposable container.

Apply the distant whitecaps with Redi-White on your liner brush. Soften the bottom edge with your round brush wet with the washing medium.

I would like to draw your attention to the fact that the two foremost waves are not very large. Starting with the most distant wave and working your way forward, one wave at a time, the technique is as follows. Apply the Redi-Gel mix where the wave is to be placed. With your fan brush, dabble phthalo blue in an irregular line under where the crest of the wave will be. Pull down slightly curved, sloping strokes from this line, leaving a lot of streaks. Fade this out on the bottom. While this is still wet, stipple Redi-White in an irregular line just above the phthalo blue with your fan brush. Immediately hook onto the bottom edge of this white with your clean, towel-dried fan brush, and pull down once again in the slightly curved, sloping stroke. Repeat all the way across the wave, leaving this very streaky, also, as you can see in figures 4. Add the foremost wave in the same manner.

Lay in the white streaks indicating water washing up on the beach, and with a brush loaded with the Redi-Gel, fade back from above with horizontal blending strokes. With a little bit of phthalo blue and Redi-Gel, place an additional hint of a shadow underneath portions of the water washing up on the beach, if needed.

STEP: 3

Flesh = CRM + CYM + Redi-White
Navy = UB + a touch of BU
Violet Gray = UB + BU + AV + RW
Black = BU + UB

Remove Art-A-Peel pattern. Paint the girl's arms and hand flesh color. Add a little BU and CRM to your dirty brush, and apply the shadows while the flesh color is still wet. Blend with a clean brush.

Add a touch of BU to some of the sky color and paint in the bottom of her sneaker. The top of the sneaker is white. After the white is dry, draw a thin gray accent line on the shoe.

Her jeans are navy, highlighted wet-on-wet with medium blue.

Paint her sweatshirt working wet-on-wet. Apply the shadows with creamy YO, and the remainder of the shirt with creamy CYM. Blend slightly, leaving dark streaks to indicate folds in the fabric. Before this dries, add an additional highlight of CYM + Redi-White to the top of the arms and between the folds on the back.

Paint in her hair using creamy BU. Quickly remove highlights, using a clean, damp angle brush. The longer curls coming down over her shoulders and back are applied with the liner brush and thin BU.

Have you contacted your television station today and thanked them for the art teaching programs?

STEP: 4

Dry your painting, and transfer or sketch your birds. Paint the birds in with the violet-gray, and highlight with Redi-White, as shown. The most distant, tiny birds are done with a liner brush double loaded with Redi-White and the violet-gray. Add the black dots for the eyes and the tips of the wings of the closer birds, including the gulls on the ground, with the liner brush. Apply their beaks and legs with YO, also using a liner brush. Cast a shadow on the ground next to the birds walking on the beach with a very watery wash of violet-gray.

The bread bag is a wash of gray, highlighted with Redi-White. After it is dry, tie a red ribbon around the top. Place a piece of bread in her hand with Redi-White.

Add some navy and water to your dark green grass color, and cast a very transparent shadow on the ground to the left of your little girl.

With your fan brush and the dark green, add additional short grasses around the little girl if you think it is needed. Lift up some taller grasses with your liner brush, using a variety of color mixtures made with the BU, dark green, YO and some CYM and Redi-White. Stipple the sea oats on the top of a few taller grasses with the fan brush using BU + Redi-White. Stipple sparse highlights on the oats with YO + Redi-White. Touch up, sign and seal.

Seal your completed paintings with a clear acrylic spray (gloss or matte) to enhance the colors and protect them. Hold the can ten to twelve inches from your canvas. With a smooth side to side motion, spray from top to bottom and back. Turn side-ways and repeat, cross-hatching the layers. Ask for a quality brand.

Go for a picnic and feed the birds!

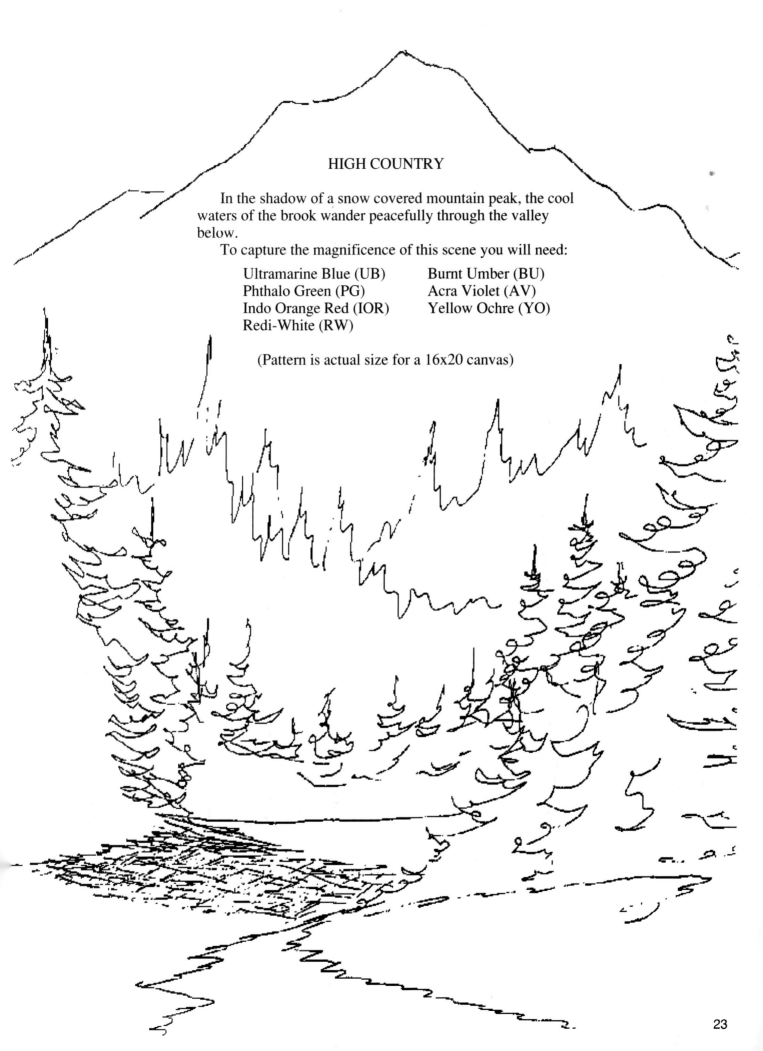

HIGH COUNTRY

In the shadow of a snow covered mountain peak, the cool waters of the brook wander peacefully through the valley below.

To capture the magnificence of this scene you will need:

Ultramarine Blue (UB)   Burnt Umber (BU)
Phthalo Green (PG)   Acra Violet (AV)
Indo Orange Red (IOR)   Yellow Ochre (YO)
Redi-White (RW)

(Pattern is actual size for a 16x20 canvas)

STEP: 1

Teal = RW + UB + PG + a touch of AV (sky&base)
Peach = RW + IOR + YO (sky)
Pink = RW + IOR + AV (mountain)
Lavender Gray = RW + UB+ BU + AV (mountain)
Dark blue-green = BU + YO + Water (tree)

Sketch the tallest mountain peak approximately 4" down from the top of a 16 x 20 canvas. The base line for the distant trees is 4" up and centered below the mountain peak.

Use your 2" blending brushes to apply the peach and teal to the sky. Use the peach to put a glow in the center behind the mountain ridge. Work the teal from the top corners down, overlapping the top edges of the peach. Blend with a towel-dried foliage stippling brush, and finish smoothing with a light touch of the fan brush.

Lighten some of both sky colors with Redi-White and lightly base coat the mountain area, and blend in the center. Mist out the bottom. (Figure 1) Apply the accent colors to the mountain with your palette knife while the base coating is still wet. Touch up with your angle brush. Blend slightly where the dark and light colors overlap. Mist out the bottom edges with your fan brush and a touch of your lightened base coat colors. (Figure 2).

Paint the remaining 4" at the bottom of the canvas with teal.

STEP: 2

Beginning about 1" below the base line, sketch in the stream. Keep the stream very small in the background, and let it get wider as it comes forward, until it widens to cover the entire bottom of the canvas. To create the "misty" depth in this painting, each row of trees should be slightly darker in value than the previous row.

The color for the most distant, barely visible, tree line is a mixture of some of your gray and teal. Hold your fan brush vertically to tap in these trees. Keep the tops ragged and vary the spacing. Mist out the bottoms of the trees with the lightened teal.

The next row of trees need to be slightly darker, so add a touch more UB and AV to some of your gray. Add the illusion of limbs staggered on either side of a few trees with the corner of the fan brush. Mist out the bottoms as before.

To create the lightest misty green trees just above the base line, add a touch of the dark blue green to some of your teal. Add more dark blue green to your dirty brush for each row of trees as you come forward.

The tall darker trees should have more detail. Lightly load the tip ends of the bristles on your fan brush. Paint only the tip top of the tree with the brush turned vertically indicate the top branches with the corner of your brush. After painting about an inch down from the top, you can safely begin to use the center portion of the fan brush to apply the branches without fear of making your tree too wide at the top. Turn the fan brush horizontally and crunch to create the illusion of longer lower limbs. Press the center of the brush on the canvas until the bristles on the outer edges of the brush barely touch the canvas to create tiny pointed edges on each limb. Stagger and zig-zag down the tree in an irregular fashion. Do not make perfectly cone shaped trees. Make each limb wider as you progress down the tree.

Should your trees become too wide, add an extra top to a wide bottom and it will become a cluster of trees rather than one huge unsightly tree.

STEP: 3

The largest dark green trees on the left side of the stream have very little teal in the dark green. To highlight the foremost tree add a touch of white to your dirty brush and sparsely apply it to the middle and left side of the tree. Leave some dark between the highlights to indicate shadows beneath each branch. For the second highlight, add some yellow ochre and more Redi-White to your dirty brush. Apply an extra sparkle of light just above the first highlight mostly on the left tips of a few branches.

The bank and the trees need to be hooked together while the dark green is still wet. Should the dark green dry before you apply the bank colors, simply add a little more green at the base of the trees and continue.

For the snow, begin with Redi-White in the center of the canvas, then switch to teal and some dark green for the shadowy area to the right of the large cluster of trees. Continue with Redi-White and teal to indicate drifts of snow on the bank.

STEP: 4

Using your fan brush and the pure dark blue green mixture, apply and highlight the dark trees on the right in the same manner as the ones on the left. Indicate a low foreground bush with the highlight colors using your bristle filbert or small foliage stippling brush.

Apply the bank while the dark color is still wet. Pull some of the dark down on the bank and highlight with Redi-White and teal.

The center of the water is peach. Around the peach is teal. The edges and the distant water is a mixture of dark green, ultramarine blue and a tiny touch of teal. Use your

angle brush to establish the outer edges of the stream only. Use your fan brush to brush the dark reflection color down and the light colors up. Overlap the edge of each color with the next, and brush a few horizontal streaks through the water with a clean towel dried fan brush. Skip a space and wipe your brush clean between each stroke. This will keep your water clean, clear and shimmery.

The bare trees and rocks are a mixture of BU, UB, AV and a tiny touch of teal, and are applied with a double loaded angle brush. Highlight with both Redi-White and pink. Touch up the bottom half of the trees with short, choppy strokes, using only one color at a time. Apply a very watery transparent shadow to the right of the trees with the dark mixture.

Make the rocks different sizes and shapes with your angle brush, and soften the bottoms where they join the snow with a clean, damp, round brush.

Streak Redi-White to the left of each tree to indicate drifts of snow.

The tree limbs and twigs on the ground are applied with a double loaded liner brush of the dark tree mixture and Redi-White. Don't forget the watery shadows on the ground to the right of each twig. All the shadows should be parallel.

Add the reflections directly underneath the trees and twigs in the water. Dampen the dried water area with clean water and paint in the reflections. Brush across the reflections with a clean brush while they are still wet to create a zig zag shimmery effect. Skip a space and wipe your brush clean between each stroke to avoid a muddy look.

Speckle your painting with both watered down Redi-White, and watered down teal (P.15)

Sign and go skiing!

Seal your painting with a clear acrylic spray to enhance the colors and protect them.

Enjoy!

Curing Time

In the "old days" tobacco was harvested, looped on sticks and hung on tier poles inside this type barn for curing. Hand labor that filled these barns has been replaced by modern machinery and the curing barn has been replaced with metal bulk barns.

This painting was designed from a photograph taken in my home town of Linden, North Carolina by Cousin Charles. To paint this vanishing breed of barn you will need:

Permanent Green Light (PGL)
Ultramarine Blue (UB)
Indo Orange Red (IOR)
Cadmium Orange (CO)
Acra Violet (AV)
Burnt Sienna (BS)
Burnt Umber (BU)
Redi-White (RW)

(Pattern is actual size for 16x20 canvas)

27

STEP: 1

Pale Tan = BU + BS + CO + a touch of UB + Redi-White
Cream = CO + Redi-White
Taupe = Pale Tan + BS + UB a touch of AV

Transfer your pattern to the canvas, positioning the peak of the barn roof 5" down from the top of your canvas, and 7" in from the left. Sketch in your horizon line 6" up from bottom in center of the canvas, and slightly lower on each side. Sketch in your road loosely with a ragged edge, slanting with a drop from 5" up from the bottom of the canvas on the left to 3" up on the right. Add the narrow path from the barn to the left side of the road.

Apply your Art-A-Peel. If you do not have an Art-A-Peel, use masking tape or a stiff piece of paper to keep your background paint from getting on the barn.

With your 2" blending brush, apply cream diagonally through the center of the sky area. Pick up pale tan on the same brush, overlap about 1/2" of the outer edges of the cream, and paint in the remainder of the sky. Using a clean, towel-dried brush, blend from the cream area out over the tan, leaving a distinct ray of light hitting the barn.

With your dirty sky brush, pick up some cream and paint in the road, working from the top down to the bottom of the canvas. Using your fan brush, pull some horizontal streaks of both taupe and BU from top of the road towards the center. Keep these streaks parallel to the bottom of the canvas to make your road lay flat.

STEP: 2

Dark Lavender Gray = BS + UB + AV + Pale Tan
Light Lavender Gray = Dark Lavender Gray + Redi-White
Dark Green = PGL + BU

Pick up some light lavender gray on your fan brush and, working one small section at a time, begin tapping in the tops of the distant trees. Immediately mist out the bottom with some of the cream from the sky. Continue working one section at a time, tapping in the tops and misting out the bottoms, until the entire tree line has been applied.

About half way between the barn and the right side of the canvas, tap in a short bushy area trailing off behind the barn. Use your fan brush and the dark lavender gray. Immediately streak some cream at the base of these trees to anchor them to the ground. Add a touch more CO to the cream and streak in a few accents to this ground area. With thinned dark lavender gray and your liner brush, lift up a few twiggy trees from the bushes.

The fall-colored bushes are painted using the watercolor technique described on page 14 in the General Instructions. The colors used are dark green, BU, BS, IOR, and AV. Apply one small section of each clump at a time. Apply the colors at random. For the bushes behind the barn and on the far side of the road, tap and wash the bottom edges out in streaks, using your clean, moist fan brush. This will create the illusion of shadows on the sand beneath the bushes. Dry and remove your Art-A-Peel.

STEP: 3

Rust = BS + IOR
Rich Brown = BU + UB + BS + AV + IOR (marbleized)

The tin roof is painted according to the wash technique described on page 15. Apply rust and wash out with a clean damp brush, leaving a sparkle of white here and there along the edge.

Underneath the shelter roof on the far side of the barn, apply rich brown at the top and rust along the bottom. Blend with a clean, damp brush. The eave is painted with the rich brown, and the rafters are applied after this dries, using taupe.

Apply a thin wash of your rich brown on the barn at the top of each section, and wash down. Work only one section at a time.

Notice the unusual shadow pattern underneath the right shelter roof. To achieve this, apply a generous amount of the rich brown and wash down at an angle across the barn on this section. Indicate the shadows from the rafters with rich brown and your liner brush. When this is dry, apply a second wash of rich brown in the shadow areas only.

After the barn is dry, intensify the color on the front with an additional wash of rich brown. Add a glow to the siding between the roof and the right shelter using a very watery wash of CO. This wash should look about like ice tea.

The fence is made with your liner brush. The most distant posts are made using taupe, and the nearer posts are a double load of taupe and rich brown. Keep the rich brown on the left side. The twiggy trees in the bushes behind the barn are taupe. The ones in the foreground are the rich brown.

The support posts under the shelters are rich brown applied with the liner brush. Apply the CO + Redi-White highlights beginning just below the brace beams. With taupe on your liner brush, apply the rafters on the broken section of the shelter roof.

STEP: 4

Using watered down taupe, add the large bare tree behind the barn with your liner and some grass around the barn and road with your fan brush. With the liner brush and the watered down rich brown, add the clapboard lines, door, and vent on the front of the barn.

Put a few posts, sticks and other "do-fers" around the barn and under the shelter. Could these be old looping horses, tobacco sticks or benches? After all, these were the old-time implements used in "barning" and curing tobacco.

With your fan brush and very watery paint, lift up sparse grasses around the barn and along the road. This technique is described in detail on page 16, figure 18. The majority of the color used is rich brown, with a little of the color from the fall bushes added.

Using your angle brush double loaded with rich brown on the bottom, and CO + Redi-White on the top, tap in rocks. Place these irregularly-sized rocks along the edge of the road, and around the barn.

With very thin taupe on your liner brush, indicate a covey of small birds in the distance. Add a few tiny twigs in any spot that seems bare. Add water to this paint for an ink-like consistency, and apply shadows behind each fence post, twig and brace beam. All shadows should be transparent and lay at the same angle throughout the painting.

Speckle sand and gravel along the road and in front of the barn, with several colors from your painting.

Sign, seal, and have a candy cigarette!

30

FLAMBOYANT FLAMINGO

Like palm trees and sunsets, the flamingo has become a symbol of Florida. Their hot pink color is a result of diet. Captive birds are fed a diet high in carotene to retain their beautiful pink color. Without this supplement their colors will soon fade.

To paint this flamboyant bird, use:

Ultramarine Blue (UB)
Cadmium Red Medium (CRM)
Cadmium Yellow Medium (CYM)
Indo Orange Red (IOR)
Redi-White (RW)

Burnt Umber (BU)
Phthalo Green (PG)
Yellow Ochre (YO)
Burnt Sienna (BS)
Redi-Gel (RG)

(Pattern is actual size for 16x20 canvas)

31

STEP: 1

Pale Peach = Redi-White + CRM + IOR + BS
Teal = Redi-White + PG + UB
Dark Green = PG + BS
Light Green = PG + BS + Redi-White
Hot Pink = CRM + IOR + Redi-White

Cover the canvas with pale peach, using the two inch blender brush. While this is still wet, add teal around all edges with the fan brush. Blend gently with your foliage stippling brush, working from the pale peach into the teal, and wiping your blending brush often. Dry completely and transfer the pattern onto the canvas, being sure to trace the logs and the reflections, also. Place the flamingo's eye approximately 6 3/4" down from the top of the canvas and 7 3/4" in from the right edge.

As I demonstrated on television, you can cover the bottom of the bird's body with Redi-Mask to protect it from the grass and log paint. Dry before applying paint.

STEP: 2

Be careful to keep the grass color off the bird and the logs. Hold a piece of heavy paper such as an index card or corner label from your Fredrix canvas over each log as you paint in that area to protect the logs from the grass paint. Use watery dark green, and BS on your fan brush for the grassy areas and reflections. If you have not masked the birds bottom, try using your angle brush around the bird and change to the fan for the outer areas. Add tall grasses and highlights with your liner brush.

With both thick and thin BU and your angle brush, begin laying in the logs with choppy, streaky strokes. Leave lots of lights and darks to indicate rough bark. Do the reflections the same way, using more watery paint, and keeping the colors much lighter. Mix some UB + BU to make an almost black shade and shadow the bottom of the upright log. With some of this dark color, paint the inside of the jagged hollows in the logs. With some BS + Redi-White, make a highlight color for the top edge of the upright log. Chop the edges of this highlight color into the darker shades to blend. Using this same color, highlight the outer edge of the hollow.

Lighten the dark green color with some Redi-White and begin putting in the distant reeds with your liner brush. Pull in some reflections at the same time. Use the photograph as a guide for placement. The reeds get darker in color as they come closer to the foreground. Double load your liner brush with BU and a highlight color (BS + Redi-White) and pull some closer reeds in, with the highlight color on the left. Begin adding a few leaves. Let some of the reeds lean to the left.

Using various shades of thinned BU and dark green, pull some curved grasses up in front of the bird and directly over the top of the upright log. Add some reed reflections on top of the reflected log, but do not put in the last of the actual reeds until the water is done.

Double load your liner brush with hot pink and Redi-White, and put in the reflections of the flamingo's legs. Do not put in the actual legs at this time, as they will be added on top of the water.

STEP: 3

Dark Blue-Green = UB + PG + a touch BU
Water Mix: Redi-Gel + Water (1 Tbsp. each) + some of the dark blue-green above (Mix this in a separate container)

With your 2" blending brush, apply the water mix across the entire water area. Work the brush back and forth horizontally. Randomly streak dark blue-green horizontally through the wet water and at the bottom of the canvas. Streak in a little of your leftover teal sky color over the reflections of the log and reeds to get a shimmery, watery look. Dry.

Add detail lines to the logs with BU and your liner brush.

Double load your liner with BU and some different highlight colors (CYM + Redi-White, BS + Redi-White, etc.), and put in the closest reeds. Hook these onto the reflections and pull up. Add more leaves, pulling a few down over the end of the upright log to add depth.

Mix a little Redi-White into the hot pink and begin basing in the flamingo's head, bill and front of neck. Pick up the hot pink and shade the bottom of the bill and head, and the back of the neck. Use photo as a guide for shadow placement, and blend the light and dark pinks together, wet on wet. Continue down the breast area with the lighter pink, adding some feathery streaks of the darker pink for variety. Apply the dark hot pink under the tail area, and define the drumstick, being sure to shade the back of each.

Double load the round brush with hot pink and Redi-White and, with white on top and pink on the bottom, begin pulling in the tail feathers. A good way to do this

is to turn the canvas sideways and, starting at the tip of the tail, pull each stroke toward you. Work right on up the back and around the wing, pulling toward the center of the bird. Let these strokes get smaller as you get closer to the neck area. With a clean, damp brush, fade out the ends of the last row of feathers to blend them into the back area near the neck.

STEP: 4

Double load your liner brush with hot pink and Redi-White and put in the legs. The white highlight is on the left side of each leg.

The eye is CYM + Redi-White, with a little hot pink on the bottom. With black, paint in the end of the bill, the nostril, the pupil of the eye, and detail under the wing. Add a small, black parenthesis on the front and back of the eye, and a white highlight in the pupil.

With some of the teal sky color, put some water lines in front of the far log. With Redi-White, add water lines around front log. Fade out the bottom of the ripples with a clean damp brush. Continue emphasizing water lines with white and teal blue. For the ripples up front fade or wash out the top edge of the white. Put in puddle around flamingo's legs. Be sure to make this puddle elongated and pointed on each end.

Sign flamboyantly! Seal and enjoy!

FINAL CATCH

Once a mighty shrimper, the "John Paul" now rests at the bottom of the sea. The sea who's bounty has been both cruel and kind to this faithful farmer of the deep. Colors needed to paint this are:

Burnt Umber (BU)
Indo Orange Red (IOR)
Burnt Sienna (BS)
Ultramarine Blue (UB)
Acra Violet (AV)
Redi-White (RW)

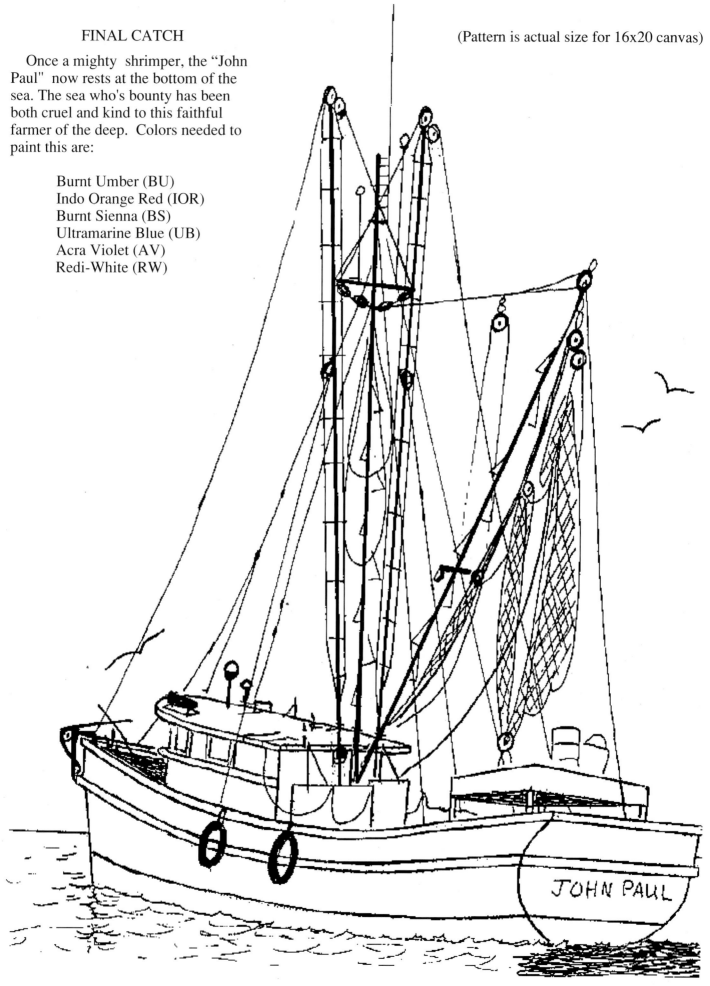

STEP: 1

Pastel Gray = UB + BU + touch of AV + RW
Very Pale Peach = IOR + RW
Violet Gray = UB + BU + AV + RW

On a 16x20 canvas draw your waterline 3 inches up from the bottom of the canvas, and transfer the hull, wheelhouse (cabin), and culling table. Do not transfer the rigging at this time. The bow of the boat, at the point it meets the water, should be 8 1/4 inches in from the left and 1/2 inch below the water line. Apply your Art-A-Peel pattern to your transfer. If you do not have an Art-A-Peel pattern, protect your transfer with masking tape.

Apply and blend the sky with both of your 2" blending brushes. Generously apply the pale peach to the center of the sky and out toward the edges, creating an irregularly shaped highlight area. Paint in the remainder of the sky with the pastel gray, making sure to overlap the outside edges of the pale peach. Blend the sky area quickly, moving from the light out and over the dark. Use a figure 8 stroke where the Redi-White and gray overlap. Create a very gradual transition between the peach and gray. Avoid muddying your sky by towel cleaning your blending brush frequently. Final blending is done with very light strokes. Continue on with the water while the sky is still wet to avoid a harsh horizon line on the left.

STEP: 2

With your fan brush streak Redi-White along the waterline. Begin at the bow of the boat and pull toward the left gradually fading the white into the gray. Do the same at the rear of the boat. This will create a shimmer along the horizon line. Blend the outer edges of the water into the sky. Apply the remainder of the water with horizontal strokes, alternating between Redi-White and pale gray. While the water is still wet, pick up some of the dark gray with your fan brush and apply it in short choppy strokes to the water area. Add a little UB to the dark gray on your brush, and chop it in. Next, pick up a very small amount of AV on the same dirty brush and apply it in the same manner. For added interest, mix a little UB + Redi-White and add some light blue ripples. Use your fan brush and some of the pastel gray, with a hint of AV added, to tap in the distant island on the right. Brush some gray and Redi-White beneath the bushes to reestablish the horizon line so that the bottom of the land mass is sitting on the water.

STEP: 3

Black = UB + BU + Water
Rust = BS + IOR
Dark Gray = BU + UB + RW
Peach = IOR + RW
Brownish-Black = Black + BU + AV

Remove your Art-A-Peel pattern, and transfer the main rigging on the boat. Carefully place your pattern on the boat so that the bottom of the main rigging is in the center of the back of the cabin. Transfer only the center mast, the two outriggers on either side, and the rear net boom. With some of your gray sky color and a little white, paint in the sky area that you can see under the culling table.

The main mast, outriggers and net boom are painted with black that is the consistency of coffee cream. Load your liner brush and start with the center mast. Hold your brush close to the bristles as if it were a pencil. Lay your hand on the canvas so that the bristles lightly touch the canvas at the top of the mast. Holding the pressure consistent from top to bottom, pull down from the elbow. This will give you a very straight, consistent line. Do the outriggers and net boom in the same manner. With the same color, add the winches, lines, net floats and cross pieces to the rigging. Paint in the shadowed areas under the roof on the side of the wheelhouse, and along the bottom side of the rails that run around the boat with the brownish-black. When applying the black to these areas, paint only a small section at a time to allow sufficient time to wash out the bottom edges. Apply the paint with your liner brush and "dabble" the bottom edge out with a very damp round brush. This gives a ragged, more realistic appearance. Shadow in the back of the wheelhouse and the bottom side of the culling table with the brownish-black. With BU, paint in the dark area inside the bow of the boat and the net boards at the base of the mast. Add some "do-fers" between the doors and the sorting table with a variety of premixed colors.

Apply the peach color to the far side of the roof of the cabin, and immediately pick up some Redi-White and apply to the near side of the roof. Blend. It shouldn't take more than one or two strokes. Touch up the black around the roof if necessary. Paint in the back of the sorting table with dark gray and the side of the table with white. Use the wash technique and dark gray on the back of the hull. Be careful not to cover up the black on the rail around the back of the boat. Add some of the dark gray to the bow of the boat and fade it in along the side. The two bumper rails around the side of the boat are painted black after the hull is completely dry.

All previous applications to the boat should be completely dry before you begin applying the following rusty areas. Apply rust on the wheelhouse just below the window, and fade or wash the color down with a clean, damp brush. Dampen the hull of the boat with clean water and apply the rusty dribbles as follows. Work one dribble area at a time. Using your liner brush, apply a cluster of rust dots and immediately dabble out the bottom edge of each one with a clean, wet, round brush. Allow the rusty paint to run down the side of the boat. After the dribbles have dried, apply the rust paint to the bottom of the boat hull. Add a shadow of BU to the rust where it meets the water, and to the rust paint on the back of the boat.

STEP: 4

Apply all the winches with black, and accent with white. The antenna on the main mast is done with a double loaded liner of dark gray and Redi-White. Apply the very thin lines with ink-like dark gray paint and your liner brush. If you like, you can apply them with a technical pen or lining tool.

The net is very thin BU with AV and IOR dabbed in. While this paint is still wet, create streaks in the paint by using a clean, damp brush to remove some paint. Dry. Crosshatch the net in one direction with ink-like dark gray and in the other with Redi-White.

The barrel on the culling table is rust highlighted with Redi-White and accented with rusty bands. Paint the bucket dark gray and use your finger to create a blotted highlight. Add the "do-fers" on top of the cabin and on the bow of the boat. Add the tires to the side with black and highlight with Redi-White.

Add a distorted reflection from the boat on the water with short choppy strokes of rust, white, peach, and gray. Soften these ripples with a clean damp brush or sponge.

The birds are done with a double loaded liner of dark gray and Redi-White. Tip the wings and dot the eye with black. Add beaks with CO.

Sign, seal, and go meet the shrimp boats!

38

ROLLING MEADOWS

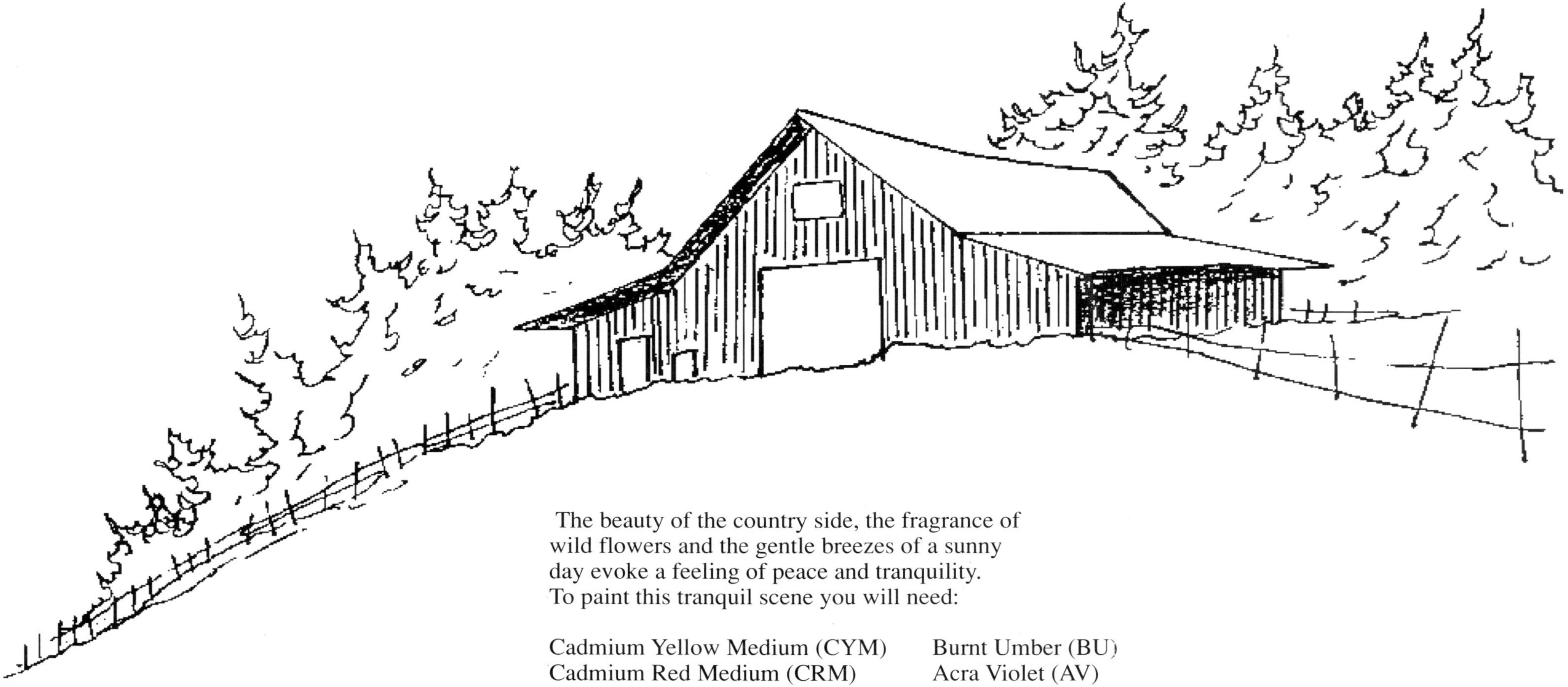

The beauty of the country side, the fragrance of wild flowers and the gentle breezes of a sunny day evoke a feeling of peace and tranquility. To paint this tranquil scene you will need:

Cadmium Yellow Medium (CYM)
Cadmium Red Medium (CRM)
Ultramarine Blue (UB)
Phthalo Green (PG)

Burnt Umber (BU)
Acra Violet (AV)
Yellow Ochre (YO)
Redi-White (RW)

(Pattern is actual size for 16x20 canvas)

STEP: 1

Light Blue = UB + Redi-White + a touch of BU
Light Pink = CRM + Redi-White
Med. Lavender Gray = UB + CRM + Redi-White
Teal = PG + UB + Redi-White
Pale Yellow = CYM + Redi-White

Transfer pattern, apply Art-A-Peel, and establish your sketch. The peak of the barn roof is 7" down from the top of the canvas, and 6 1/4" in from the right. Sketch the hill as shown underneath the barn. It slopes down to a valley on the left that is 3" up from the bottom of the canvas. The distant hills are about an inch taller than the meadow line.

The clouds in the top of the sky are larger and more billowing than those in the bottom. Work in one small section of the sky at a time to allow plenty of time for blending, but do not allow any section to dry before moving on to the next. You will be working wet-on-wet, wetting only one section at a time, sometimes using color, sometimes using Redi-White as per the following instructions.

Begin with the light blue at the top of the sky. Immediately overlap the bottom of the blue with Redi-White loaded on the corner edge of the large 2" brush. Blend with an erratic stroke of the foliage stippling brush to give a loose, blustery look. With Redi-White on the corner of your fan brush, define the top edges of a few clouds in this blustery area, and blend out the bottom edges. Do not allow this to dry before continuing to scrub in more Redi-White under these clouds. Keep the bottom edge of this irregular to avoid a straight line across your canvas.

Apply some of the premixed sky colors at random, using the photo as a placement guide, and blend with your foliage stippling brush. Once again, define the top edges of some white clouds just below these colorful accents. An occasional gray cloud here or there will add some interest, also. Be sure to fade out the bottom edges. At the bottom of the sky, apply Redi-White and loosely blend some

lavender gray into this, leaving a streaky, undefined look.

Do not go back into any part of the sky that has begun to dry and set up, as you will remove the paint and spots of the canvas will begin to show through. Should you need to touch up, do so after it is completely dry, using the wet-on-dry technique (Page 12).

Use lavender-gray on the corner of your fan brush, turned vertically, and tap in the illusion of a few treetops and the right side of the far distant hill. Highlight the left side with light yellow and blend. Add a little teal to your dirty brush, and repeat the same procedure for the next hill. Intensify this color with a touch of AV and PG, and indicate small, distant trees on the foreground hill.

STEP: 2

Dark Green = BU + PG + UB
Rust = BU + CRM

With the corner of your fan brush held vertically, tap in the dark green trees around the barn. Add YO + Redi-White to your dirty brush, and tap in highlights on the top and left side of a few trees. To this dirty brush, add CRM and AV, and tap in additional accent colors.

Remove your Art-A-Peel pattern. The roof of the barn is done with rust, using the wash technique as explained on Page 15. Apply a very light wash of BU on the front of the barn, and a heavier wash on the right side. Deepen the color with a little BU + UB, and add the windows, doors, and eaves after the first wash is dried. With very watery BU on your liner brush, add clapboard and tin roof lines.

STEP: 3

Dusty Blue-Green = PG + AV + a touch of BU + Redi-White
Warm Yellow = YO + Redi-White

Work the ground area a section at a time, using a wet-on-wet technique. The hill immediately under the barn is worked first, and the foreground rise is worked next.

Smear a thin undercoat beginning in the central portion of the hilltop, using your 2" blending brush and some dusty blue-green. Add touches of your sky and tree colors to vary this undercoat. Add BU to this basecoat color, and zigzag a little gully down the hill.

Once again beginning in the central portion of the hill, highlight with a fan brush lightly loaded with warm yellow. Hold the fan brush with the bristles up, and the handle down and almost flat against the canvas. Flap the flat side of the brush against the canvas. Change highlight colors as you move around in the grassy area. I used some of all the colors from the sky to do this. To give the hill a rounded appearance, subdue the highlight colors near the gully with some of the dusty blue-green.

STEP: 4

Base in the right foreground portion of the hill, using some of your dusty blue-green at the top, and adding BU and some of the dark green as you work forward. The highlights in this area are applied using the meadow grass technique described on Page 16. Begin with your fan brush, holding the brush perpendicular to the canvas, and crunch short highlights at the top of this hill. Switch to the 2" blending brush as you move down. Once again, use a variety of shades.

The bushes in the left corner and across the front are tapped in with the sponge, using dark green. Tap these bushes in while the grass is still wet so there is no separation between these bushes and the grass on the right portion of the hill. There is a distinct separation between the bushes and the grass immediately behind them.

Highlight the bushes with warm yellow, and begin adding distinct patches of wild flowers with CRM + CYM, CRM + AV, CRM + Redi-White. Do not cover all of your darks. Add daisies in a variety of colors.

The foreground fence posts are BU with a touch of UB. They are applied with short, choppy strokes of the angle brush, creating texture. Highlight on the left with choppy strokes of pink and light yellow.

Add a touch of gray to the dark fencepost color. Double load your liner brush with this color and light pink, and put in the distant fence. Notice that the fenceposts are taller as they come down the hill, to make them appear closer.

Sign and go for a hike in the country!

To enhance the colors and protect your finished painting, seal it with a clear acrylic spray. Have a great day!

BUCK FEVER

The white-tailed deer is a delight to see a field, graceful in movement, a ballet artist on an outdoor stage.

Deer hunting is the subject of more heated arguments than any other sport, and has caused the passage of more laws and regulations than one can count. I understand that this animal drives hunters to climb trees, sleep in bitter cold, get lost, brag and boast, start fights, even get divorces.

No matter what your conviction or stand on the issue, I think we all agree that the white-tailed deer epitomizes nature's joy, grace and beauty. The deer is truly "dear" to all of us!

To paint this majestic buck, prepare!

Cadmium Yellow Medium (CYM)   Burnt Umber (BU)
Ultramarine Blue (UB)   Acra Violet (AV)
Phthalo Green (PG)   Yellow Ochre (YO)
Hookers Green (HG)   Redi-Gel (RG)
Redi-White (RW)

(Pattern is actual size of 16x20 canvas)

STEP: 1

Clear = 1 Tbsp. Redi-Gel + 2 Tbsp. water (Mix this in a disposable container)
Dusty Blue-Green = UB + HG + Redi-White.
Dark Blue-Green = A marbleized mixture of UB, HG, BU and a touch of AV.
Taupe = BU + Redi-White with a touch of UB and AV.

Paint a 16 x 20 canvas with black latex or acrylic paint. Two thin coats crosshatched works much better than one heavy application. Dry thoroughly after each application.

Generously apply the Redi-Gel mixture over the entire canvas with your 2" blending brush. Quickly brush a thin coating of the marbleized mixture over the top 3/4 of the canvas in the tree area.

With your fan brush and some of the dusty blue-green, apply a hazy mist at the base of the trees. The stroke is an erratic crisscross applied loosely in an up and down, back and forth, "every which way but loose" manner. With an erratic crisscross stroke, apply another layer of mist with the taupe just below the previous dusty blue-gray mist. This will join the blue-gray mist area to the dark umber color below.

Apply BU to the wet Redi-Gel at the bottom of the canvas, coming up about 3" on the right side and 2" on the left. Add random streaks of UB near the bottom of the BU, and random streaks of AV near the top of the BU. Brush back and forth to blend these colors on the canvas.

With your sponge, apply the dusty blue-green randomly over the dark tree background, creating texture to give the illusion of trees. Add additional highlights to indicate individual trees in the upper portion of the canvas. Do not

make these highlights too symmetrical.

Highlight a few of the upper trees using your dirty sponge and YO. Add a touch of CYM to your dirty sponge and apply the final highlight to the top of one or two trees. Dry completely.

STEP: 2

Warm Brown = BU + a touch of UB and Redi-White
Golden Brown = YO + Redi-White with a touch of BU and AV

NOTE: Add enough water to each color used on the deer to give the paint the consistency of Redi-White.

Position your deer pattern so that the eye is 8" up from the bottom, and 4 1/2" in from the left side of the canvas. Tape your pattern in place and trace the deer with white Saral, wax-free transfer paper. Should you incur smudges outside the design, remove the excess after your painting is completely dry with either a kneaded eraser or a damp sponge.

The deer is painted with a wet-on-wet technique. The darker color is applied with an angle brush, and the highlight color is applied with a liner brush. A clean, towel-dried round brush is then used to blend the two colors together to achieve a softly graduated shading. The rich look of this deer's coat requires at least two applications of paint. Quickly brush on and blend one application of the light and dark colors, establishing your shadows and highlights. Dry completely and reapply as many coats as necessary to achieve the desired effect. It is important to work only one small section of the deer at a time. I began with the antlers, which I applied with a

double loaded liner brush. I then applied one ear at a time, blending each before moving on to the head, the neck, the body area, and each individual leg.

STEP: 3

Light Golden Brown = Golden Brown + YO + Redi-White
Light Blue-Gray = UB + Redi-White + a touch of BU

After the deer is dry, apply a line of light golden brown on the top of his face, and tap and fade out with a clean, moist round brush. Continue working one section at a time in this manner to add a sparkle of light to the deer's chest, back, and left legs.

The light fur areas are applied with short choppy strokes of the liner brush, using light blue-gray. Each stroke should be applied in the direction that the fur lays on the deer. Notice the amount and placement of this color in the figure above.

Randomly tap foliage over the dark ground cover, using your sponge and all of the premixed colors on your palette, except blue-gray. Apply the darker tones first, and the lighter colors in the foreground. Be sure to tap a little of the dark colors over the deer's feet to tuck them in.

Thank you for contacting your television program director in support of my art teaching programs!

STEP: 4

Black = UB + BU

Pull up some taller grasses with your liner brush using a variety of the colors from the ground cover. You will need to add additional water to your paint to make these grassy strokes. Indicate a few definite leaves at random on the tips of some of the grasses, and here and there throughout the foliage. Using a fan or tooth brush, lightly speckle the lower section of the grass highlights with taupe, warm brown, and golden brown.

Sparsely apply Redi-White highlights with the liner brush to the light blue-gray areas on the deer. Refer to the figure above for the exact placement of these highlights, and remember to place these strokes in the direction that the fur grows. Many areas of the blue-gray, such as the ears, tummy, and legs, only have two or three tiny dots of the Redi-White. The Redi-White is applied at an angle on the neck, leaving a shadow under the head. Place a few strokes on top of the nose and in front of the eye. He should have a very prominent bright white chin.

With your thinned black paint and a liner brush, paint in a round pupil with a curved line over the top (☜). Place a smaller dot under the eyelid on the far side. Apply the black nose and the line for the mouth. The dark spot of fur behind the nose and above the mouth is made with charcoal (black + a touch of Redi-White). After the black has dried, add a highlight dot of Redi-White in each eye and on the nose.

Sign, seal, and go for a stroll in the woods.

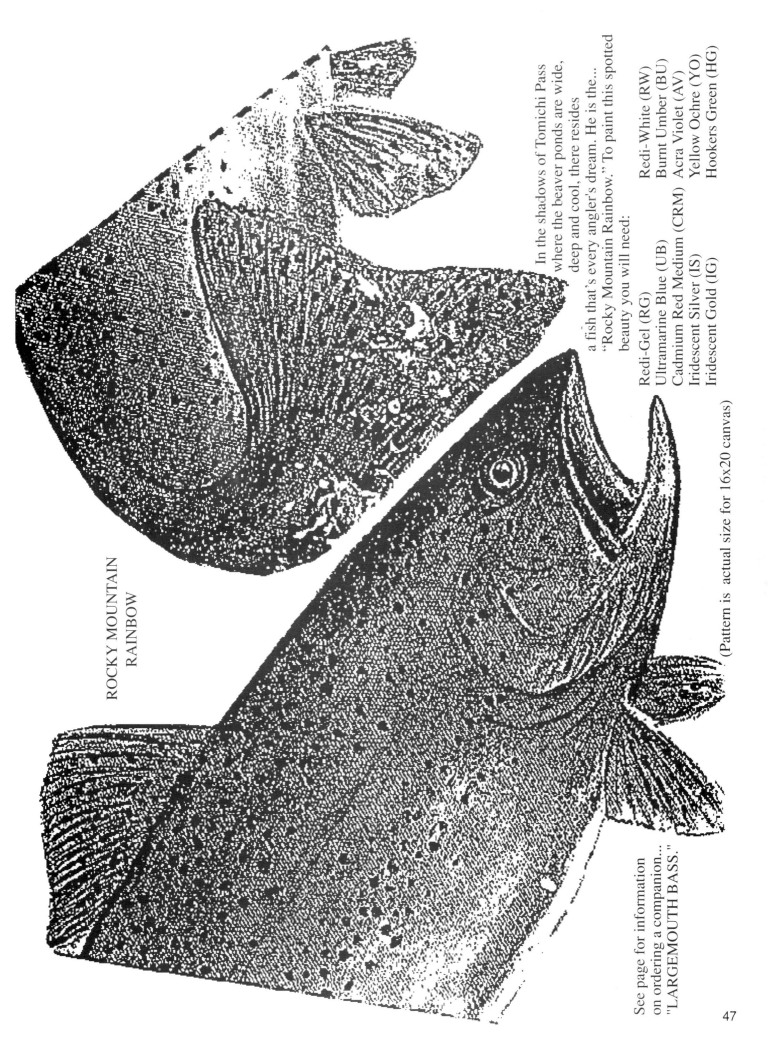

ROCKY MOUNTAIN
RAINBOW

In the shadows of Tomichi Pass where the beaver ponds are wide, deep and cool, there resides a fish that's every angler's dream. He is the... "Rocky Mountain Rainbow." To paint this spotted beauty you will need:

Redi-Gel (RG)	Redi-White (RW)
Ultramarine Blue (UB)	Burnt Umber (BU)
Cadmium Red Medium (CRM)	Acra Violet (AV)
Iridescent Silver (IS)	Yellow Ochre (YO)
Iridescent Gold (IG)	Hookers Green (HG)

(Pattern is actual size for 16x20 canvas)

See page for information on ordering a companion... "LARGEMOUTH BASS."

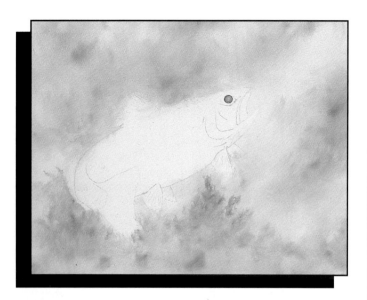

STEP: 1

Light Cream = Redi-White + YO
Yellow Green = YO + HG + UB
Navy = 4 parts UB + 1 part BU
Blue-Green = UB + HG
Peach = Redi-White + CRM + YO
Black = UB + BU (equal parts)
Gray = Blue-Green + Redi-White + AV
Orange = YO + CRM
Aqua = Phthalo Green + a touch of UB

Transfer your pattern to the canvas. The center of the trout's eye should be located 5 3/4" down from the top of the canvas, and 7 1/2" in from the right side. Begin covering the background with the light cream color. With your fan brush, randomly tap in splotches of your dark green, some UB, YO and a few little touches of AV and PG. Quickly blend the colors into the cream with a foliage stippling brush. Leave the background blustery with a lot of cream showing. It may be helpful to work in small sections, referring to the photograph for placement of these shades. Avoid getting paint on your fish. Wipe your blending brush often as you work to avoid getting muddy colors.

Mix a little of your navy with the light cream to get a dusty blue-gray. Load only one corner of your fan brush with the gray and, holding the brush vertically with the loaded corner up, crunch the brush in erratic directions to indicate the splash under the fish and behind his tail.

Circle inside the eye with orange. Immediately fill the center in with YO, and put a dot of Redi-White in the center of this. Tap blend these wet colors from the center out with a clean towel-dried round brush to give the eye a protruding look. When completely dry, add a black pupil in the middle, and a white highlight towards the upper front of the pupil.

STEP: 2

Clear = Redi-Gel + water

Apply some Redi-Gel plus water to the dorsal fin of the fish, using the fan brush. While this clear gel is still wet, pull some of your yellow green down from the outer edge of the fin, and pull some dark blue green up from the base of the fin. Leave it transparent. The fish looks best if you apply 2 thin layers of Redi-Gel and paint, drying between each application.

Begin basing the body of the fish with Redi-Gel and a little water. (Do not begin working the curved tail section at this time.) While the gel is still wet, begin laying in the stripes of color, beginning with the dark blue green along the spine, and in front of tail to create a shadow in the curve between the tail and body sections. Fade the edge of this shadow in with your fan brush. Keep this dark green stripe about 1/4" wide. Lay in the yellow-green stripe next and fade out with a clean angle brush. Lay in stripes of watered down blue, aqua, AV, a glow of pink, all softened together with your angle brush. These colors stop just below the center of the body. Add Redi-White just below the pink and along the bottom edge of the trout with a shadow of violet gray blended in between.

With your lavender gray shadow color, shade behind the gills.

Using liner brush, put a blue green line around eye, and fade back with a clean, round brush. Skip a small space and add a blue green half circle for emphasis, and fade back with the round brush. Underneath the eye, add a larger half circle to emphasize the eye socket. Fade this upward. Outline the left side of the lip with this same color and add some yellow green in the center, and on the bottom lip. Remove some color from the center with a clean brush to leave a glow.

Apply peach to the front of the mouth, and a blue-green shadow inside the mouth, and blend together. Accent the

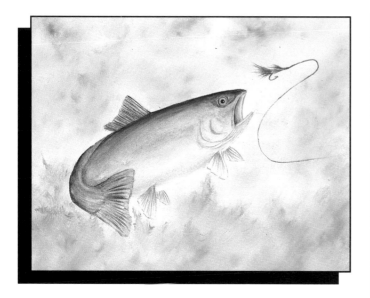

outside edge with a soft line of blue green.

Recoat gill area with Redi-Gel, deepen shadows under gills, and add AV in front of gill slits and on gill plate. With your liner brush and the lavender gray, add accent lines on gills. Accent between these lines with Redi-White.

Apply Redi-Gel to lower fins, and brush peach from the outer edges toward the trout's body. Using blue-gray and your liner brush, streak in the fin rays, working from the body of the fish toward the outer edge of the fin.

STEP: 3

Apply Redi-Gel to the tail and tail fin. Highlight the top edge of the tail with yellow-green. Use your dark blue-green on the outside edge of the fish from the dorsal fin to the tail fin. Work your AV and aqua stripes into the center of the tail section. At the base of the tail fin begin streaking in some blue-green with the chisel edge of your angle brush. Work from the base of the tail fin towards the edge. Apply some yellow-green along the outside edge of the tail fin and fade back towards the body. With your liner brush, add the tail fin rays with some blue-green, working from the base of the tail fin towards the edge. Accent the rays in the dorsal fin with this same color.

If necessary, reapply Redi-Gel and intensify colors on the fish where needed. Sharpen up any accent lines in the fins that need emphasis.

The fly is made with your liner brush, AV and PG. With your liner brush pull out longer feathers and overstroke a few of them with Redi-White while still wet. With your liner brush, add the hook and line with ink-like blue-green.

STEP: 4

Lighten your aqua with some Redi-White, and pick up a little on the corner of your fan brush. Tap in a little splash shape over the tail and behind the fish.

Pick up Redi-White on the corner of the fan brush and, holding the brush vertically, begin scrunching in the white splashy highlights above the blue and aqua splashes of water around the fish. Do this in a very irregular, zigzag pattern. Dip your liner brush handle into the Redi-White and make some dots of water here and there at the end of the splashes. Be sure to pull some splashes up in front of the tail and lower fins to make the fish look as though it is just leaping up out of the water.

With some of the black on the tip of your round brush, begin placing spots on the fish, using the picture as your guide. Notice these spots are heavier on the dark green part of the back and on the tail fin. Gray this color down with some Redi-White and place spots on the lower fins.

If you wish, after the fish is dry, brush some Redi-Gel and water along the backbone of the trout, and swish some watery Iridescent Gold or Metallic Gold acrylic paint very thinly along this dark area. Repeat with silver on his tummy and bottom fins. If necessary, reapply black over any spots that are dulled by this step. Redi-Gel mixed with bronzing powder will work well for this technique, also.

Sign, seal, and go for your cold water catch of the day!

Write for a companion project packet titled "Largemouth Bass."

49

MUM'S THE WORD

Chrysanthemums set the stage for fall with a backdrop of lavish color. This perennial blooms in a broad scope of colors, tones and shades. Each plant produces a myriad of blooms. Cut as many as you want: you will leave a throng of garden gems behind. To paint this bouquet you will need:

Ultramarine Blue (UB) Burnt Umber (BU)
Yellow Ochre (YO) Burnt Sienna (BS)
Cadmium Yellow Medium (CYM) Acra Violet (AV)
Chrome Oxide Green (COG) Phthalo Green (PG)
Hookers Green (HG) Redi-White (RW)

(Pattern is actual size for 16x20 canvas)

(Flowers are the actual size I used. Add more, and move flowers around to make your design fit the size surface you choose.)

STEP: 1

Bright Yellow = CYM + RW
Medium Yellow = YO + RW
Turquoise = PG + RW
Medium Blue = UB + RW
Medium Violet = AV + RW
Medium Green = Chrome Oxide Green + RW
Dark Green = Hookers Green + BU

NOTE: Before beginning the background on this painting, it is helpful to indicate placement of the mums. An easy way to avoid losing your sketch under the paint is to stick a piece of masking tape in the middle of each flower. These are easy to remove after the background is dry, and will leave a white spot where each mum goes. Then resketch or paint around the spot.

Scrub Redi-White into the top section of the canvas on an angle. The Redi-White will come down about 3/4 of the way on the left side and nearly half way down on the right. While this is still wet, apply some bright yellow in the center portion of the background and a little medium yellow randomly around it. Blend quickly. Immediately begin tapping in various colors around the border with your fan brush, and blend them gently with your 2" blending, foliage stippling, or fan brush. Towel clean or change your blending brush frequently to avoid muddy colors. Follow the photographs for placement and do not overblend. Begin to darken the lower part of the background on each side with burnt sienna and acra violet. Should your top section be too dry to blend at this time, reapply some Redi-White and the color adjacent to where the dark is to join and blend. Hook the bottom of this reddish brown color to burnt umber for the bottom of the background. Squeeze some BU directly onto the bottom of your canvas and brush out horizontally, using a very moist blending brush. Blend in a few streaks of AV and UB while this is still wet. Darken the areas between the mums with dark green, and while this color is still wet, pick up a little YO on your sponge and tap over it, working

out over the edges to create some very soft "ferny" areas. Add the shapes of a few leaves with the dark green and highlight a few with yellow ochre mixed with a touch of white. Dry before adding the mums.

STEP: 2

Violet Blue = AV + UB

Remove masking tape. Paint one flower at a time, working wet-on-wet. Apply an acra violet oval the approximate size you wish your mum to be over the spot marked. Working quickly so that the paint remains very wet, add a tiny shadow area of violet blue where the center of the flower is going to be, and another shadow area along the bottom right side of this oval. (See figure #1). Immediately begin laying in the petals with a round brush and Redi-White, continuing to work wet on wet. The first row of petals surround the dark center of the flower (see figure #2), then come down the sides of the flower. To do the row of petals along the bottom of the flower, double load your brush with AV and Redi-White and pull them into the bottom of the AV oval. Continue to add rows of white petals, overlapping each (figure #3), always working wet on wet. Finally, crisscross the last row of petals over the point where the petals on the "bowl" of the flower overlap the petals on the "skirt" of the flower. It is important to remember that this is all done wet on wet.

Dry time on the mum petals is quite lengthy as the Redi-White stays wet a long time when it is thick. Therefore, do not keep going over your flower as you will get a blob. You must retain the light, medium, and dark contrast. After the flowers are dry you can touch up the tips of a few petals or even add a few with a double loaded

STEP: 4

Continue to highlight leaves with YO + Redi-White. Using very watery paint, pull in a few transparent leaves in the background with leaf green. Pull out a few more twigs and "grassy" shapes. If you want to add a little pizzazz to your painting, add a few highlights to your leaves with some turquoise and medium violet. Double load a round or angle brush with some of the turquoise and medium violet, and put in some one-stroke filler leaves.

Step back and check your painting. Add those final highlights and accents to make it really special. Sign. To enhance the colors and to protect your painting, spray it with a clear acrylic sealer. I used the gloss for this one.

Chrysanthemums come in an array of colors. Why not practice these, and try some in your favorite color!

Share your bouquet with someone special!

brush or Redi-White. If this is not sufficient, you can wait until all the Redi-White is dry, inside out, and apply an ink like wash of acra violet over an area of a flower for shadow, or a base for a few accent petals over an overworked area.

The smaller flowers are done in a similar manner, starting with AV applied in a cup shape with a ragged outer edge which is darkened with UB. (See Figure #1). Again, pull a row of petals down with Redi-White, and add the petals around the bottom of the flower with a double load of AV and Redi-White.

The three filler flowers underneath the largest mum are done with the violet blue and are not in as much detail. After these dry you may wish to tap a little watery dark green over the base of them to recess them.

STEP: 3

Leaf Green = Chrome Oxide Green + BU

Put in the flower stems with very thin dark green using your liner brush. Add some twigs and branches with BU and BU + Redi-White. With very creamy leaf green and your angle brush, begin laying in more basic leaf shapes, working from the outside edge of each leaf toward the center. Begin to apply some highlights in the same manner, using YO mixed with a touch of Redi-White. Add a few grass like strokes springing forth out of the bouquet with several shades of watery paint.

PALM HAMMOCK

Early in this century the American Egret faced extinction because its feathers were in great demand within the garment industry. Laws were enacted to protect them and they made a dramatic come back, however; they now face a new and just as devastating adversary. Toxic waste pouring into our wet lands again threatens their very existence.

To capture the grace and charm of this great bird you will need:

Indo Orange Red (IOR)   Burnt Umber (BU)
Cadmium Yellow Medium (CYM)   Burnt Sienna (BS)
Chromium Green Oxide (CGO)   Yellow Ochre (YO)
Ultramarine Blue (UB)   Hookers Green (HG)
Phthalo Green (PG)   Redi-White (RW)

(Pattern is actual size of 16x20 canvas)

STEP: 1

Pale Peach = RW + IOR + a touch of YO
Light Blue = RW + UB + speck of BU

The water line is 5" up from the canvas bottom, and the horizon line is 1" above that. Cover the sky area with the pale peach color using your 2" blending brush and add the light blue streaks in the top left corner, down and across the sky. Blend slightly.

Use your same pale peach and pull down from the water line, covering about half the water area in an irregular pattern. Lift up from the bottom of the canvas with the light blue. With a clean, towel-dried brush, blend back and forth across the water area. Do not overblend. Leave light and dark areas.

STEP 2:

Med. Brown = BU + a little UB + a touch of Redi-White
Bright Peach = IOR + CYM + Redi-White
Light Gray = Pale Peach + Light Blue

With your fan brush, tap in the most distant trees. Lift up a few twiggy tree shapes with your liner brush and tap some foliage onto the tops of these trees.

Add some COG and BU to the tree color and tap in the middle distance trees on the left. Using a mixture of YO and Redi-White, streak some distant marsh grass across the canvas, adding some BU streaks here and there for variety. This will add depth to your painting.

The central clump of bushes is a mixture of COG, BU, BS and a little IOR mixed and tapped on with the sponge. After the water area is dry, dampen with clean water and your sponge. Tap in the reflections under your clump of bushes, using the same color with some UB added. Take your clean fan brush and brush this reflection down lightly. Wipe the brush, and streak back and forth horizontally to shimmer the reflection. Wipe away any streaking around the edge of the reflected bushes with your clean moist sponge leaving a nice, soft edge around the reflection. The reflection should be thin and transparent.

Highlight the central clump of bushes with your sponge using YO and a touch of the dark bush paint. Tap it onto the top and right sides of the bushes. Add some white to the YO and tap in a second highlight.

Using the fan brush, pull up additional marsh grasses, alternating layers of YO and BS, with a little BU on the left. Pull down for the reflection of the grasses.

For the palm trunks and the spikes on each side, double load your liner brush with med. brown and bright peach. Pull down the bottom layer of old palm fronds with this same color. Add the remainder of the palm fronds with the green color used in the central bushes. Each palm frond originates from the center of the tree, and consists of a stem with a fan shaped "leaf" at the end. These fronds overlap each other every which way. The first highlight color for the palm fronds is made with your dirty liner brush and YO. Add more white and YO to this color for your second highlight.

STEP 3:

Teal = UB + Phthalo green + BU + a touch of RW

Use your sponge to mix and apply the dark rich green foreground trees and bushes in the bottom left corner (HG, BU, BS, UB & IOR). Dampen the dried water area with clean water before adding the reflection. Add some UB to the dark green color, and still using the sponge, pull straight down for the reflection.

To highlight these bushes, add some YO to the sponge and lightly tap the outer edges. For the second highlight, add more YO and a touch of Redi-White to this and highlight the tip ends of only a few of the bushes.

Tap sparse reflected light on the bushes with the teal, using your sponge. Keep this color dull. If it gets too bright, tap in some of your original green color over it.

STEP 4:

Dusty Gray = Redi-White + BU + UB + COG

Using a liner brush double loaded with creamy BU and bright peach, add branches to the foreground foliage. With watery BU add in smaller branches and twigs.

With dusty gray on your fan brush, start the clumps of Spanish Moss on the foreground trees. Switch to your liner brush to complete the detail on this moss.

Add some YO highlights to the bush in the left foreground, but don't overdo. This bush is in the shadows. Using your liner brush and various shades of green and brown, pull some tall grasses up from this clump.

Using BU and your angle brush, lay in the river bank and highlight with BS and Redi-White.

Streak water lines through the bright section of water with Redi-White on your liner brush. Shimmer them by lightly brushing horizontally with your finger. Add some UB to the white for the water lines in the shadowy area.

Dry your canvas completely and transfer the bird using white graphite paper. Basecoat the bird with some of your left-over blue sky color and dry. Highlight the bird with white along the top of the head and neck, the top of the back, and the front of the wing. With a clean, damp, round brush, soften the edges of this white into the blue-gray to blend. The only crisp white edge should be on the bottom of the bird's wing, above the gray on his upper legs.

The beak and eye are painted with YO and highlighted with a CY and Redi-White mixture. Using black and the liner brush, put parentheses around the eye area, and a pupil in the center. The legs are painted black, with a subtle highlight on the back of each leg done with the blue-gray color from the bird's body.

Paint the bird's reflection distortedly using the same colors. Zigzag across the reflection with the fan brush. With some blue-gray and white, add circles in the water around his feet and legs between the bird and its reflection.

Check your painting and add or subtract if necessary. Sign, seal, and go bird watching!

PIGEON POINT LIGHTHOUSE

On the beautiful Pacific coastland stands Pigeon Point Lighthouse. It has guided mariners between Santa Cruz and Half Moon Bay since 1872. Its 115 foot tower is one of the tallest on the Pacific Coast.

To paint this coastal beauty, you will need:

Cadmium Red Medium (CRM)   Burnt Umber (BU)
Ultramarine Blue (UB)   Hookers Green (HG)
Phthalo Green (PG)   Acra Violet (AV)
Yellow Ochre (YO)   Redi-White (RW)

(Pattern is actual size of 16x20 canvas)

STEP 1:

Blue-Gray = UB + BU + RW
Lt. Blue = Blue-Gray + UB + RW
Gray = UB + CRM + RW
Violet = AV + RW
Pink = CRM + RW
Teal = UB + PG + RW

Transfer your pattern to the canvas. The peak of the lighthouse is 2 1/4 inches down and 7 inches in from the right of your canvas. The horizon line is 3 3/4 inches up from the bottom. Apply your Art-A-Peel pattern to the lighthouse. If you paint your sky before you transfer your pattern, when the sky is dry, paint the lighthouse and cottages with Redi-White, and dry before you apply the colors. If you don't white out these areas, you will not get sharp clear colors when it's time to detail them.

Make the clouds and highlights larger and more prominent in the top of the sky. The activity in the bottom half should be very subtle.

Work in one section of the sky at a time. Begin your sky in the upper left corner. Pick up some of the blue-gray with your 2 inch blending brush. Apply it in an irregular cloud-like shape (pg. 10). Using a different brush, quickly overlap the bottom of the blue-gray with light blue. Using small, circular, continuous strokes, push Redi-White up from the bottom overlapping the blue-gray approximately 1/4 inch. Blend and shape the edges of the clouds with a clean towel-dried foliage stippling or fan brush. Use the same technique to do the sky in the right corner. Alternate between the gray and Redi-White to separate the large billowing clouds and to place clouds in front of clouds. Blend as before. While this is still wet, pick an area in the white clouds that you would like to accent, apply the teal and blend into the surrounding wet paint. Do the same with a hint of all the pre-mixed sky colors.

Paint in the remainder of the sky down to the water line with streaks of both light blue and Redi-White. Blend each section of the sky together leaving no stopping and starting points. While still wet, randomly add in some of

the violet, teal, pink and gray. Blend, using left to right strokes slanting upwards at the right end. Do not overblend as the variation of colors and shades adds interest.

STEP 2:

Phthalo blue = UB + PG
Blue Violet = UB + a touch AV

After the background sky is dry, highlight only a few spots on the outer edges of the basic cloud formation. Highlight only one little puff on a cloud at a time. Tap Redi-White on the outside edge of the basic cloud formation with the corner of your fan brush. Fade or scumble out the bottom and inside edges with a clean, very moist bristle filbert brush. Skip around alternating between pink and Redi-White. Leave lots of little bumps and irregularities on the top edges of the cloud highlight.

For the clouds inside the basic cloud, tap Redi-White or pink just below a spot of color and scumble out as before.

For the tiny clouds in the lower part of the sky, tap the Redi-White slightly above the gray and scumble out leaving a shadowy bottom edge to indicate a breeze just above the water.

Be sure to work only one small section of a cloud at a time, scumble out the bottom edge, and do not highlight all the way around each cloud.

The water is worked wet-into-wet, using the techniques for whitecaps and waves described in the general instructions on page 13. Start with the light blue color at the horizon line. Begin adding the teal, gray, and dark premixed colors above as you come forward in the water. About an inch down from the horizon line, add the small rock on the left. The rock is some of the dusty blue-gray from the top of the sky with a little bit of BU brushed over it. It is highlighted with white and a little bit of pink from the sky.

Add more water and hook it onto the rock. The colors should get darker as you work closer to the beach. Add the larger foreground waves.

The beach is some of the violet-gray from the sky with a little umber mixed for the sand. After the sand is dry, streak a slightly angled line of Redi-White across it to indicate where the water is washing up on the beach. Brush and fade out the top edge of this with perfectly parallel horizontal strokes.

STEP 3:

Black = BU + UB

The top of the lighthouse is CRM and is shadowed along the back with BU and UB. The windows are blocked in with the sky colors and Redi-White. The lighthouse is Redi-White with a violet gray (blue-gray + AV) shadow on the right side. Blend quickly with a towel-dried brush, using vertical strokes. After this is dry, brush a little light yellow (RW+YO) over the left side.

The details on the lighthouse are black. You can use a technical pen with India ink, a lining tool or watery black paint on your liner brush. You might want to sketch the railings or use a tracing paper pattern before you begin. Highlight with Redi-White where shown in step 4. The side window is applied with watered down umber, and is blotted with your finger while wet to remove some of the paint, to indicate reflected light.

For the roof of the cottage, loosely mix together some BU, CRM and Redi-White. Leave the color marbleized. Lightly load your angle brush, hold the brush horizontally and tap the roof of the cottage to indicate shingles. Emphasize the shingles with some additional BU tapped in. Add a little more Redi-White to the basic color for the roof of the cottage stoop. Add a little more CRM to this

color for the roofs of the houses in back. Add the chimneys with these same mixtures.

Shadow the houses with a tan wash (RW + BU) and highlight with light yellow (RW + YO). Add the black details after the house is dry. The eaves of the houses are tan and the exhaust stack is gray highlighted with Redi-White.

STEP: 4

Dark Green = HG = BU

Using BU with a lot of water, streak on the large rocks (2" & Fan). This paint should be thick and thin creating light and dark areas. Add gray streaks of reflected light in the wet BU on right side of the rock mass. Randomly add a little watery AV to the rocks to add interest. Highlight front of the rocks on the left of the mass with the pink from the sky.

While the rocks are still wet, take a little of the gray sand color and streak it horizontally into the bottom of the rocks to hook the rocks to the ground. When the rocks are dry, add additional shadows in the crevices with a BU wash and highlight as needed.

Tap in the grass with the dark green and your fan brush. Hold your fan brush with the handle pointing down, keep the bristles flat against the canvas, and flap. While the grass is still wet, highlight with YO + Redi-White. You are just aiming for a textured look. Avoid getting too much height in the grass.

The fence and birds are done with a double loaded liner brush of gray and white. Add some black to the wing tips of several birds. Sign!

61

WOODIE ON THE WING

The wood duck is a favorite of many sportsmen. Maybe it is because the colors and markings on this waterfowl are breathtakingly beautiful. Show your unique colors when you paint this bird! In this text, I used the following colors:

Burnt Umber (BU)   Redi-White (RW)
Burnt Sienna (BS)   Redi-Mask (RM)
Ultramarine Blue (UB)   Hookers Green (HG)
Cadmium Red Medium (CRM) Yellow Ochre (YO)

(Pattern is actual size for 16x20 canvas)

STEP: 1

I want to share with you an endless source of ideas for paintings—your local wallpaper store. This particular pattern came from the wallpaper book entitled "American Gentlemen Vol. II." The actual coloring of the duck in this sample is taken from the border print that coordinated one of their major lines of wall coverings. The border print colors were shades of earth tones and blues, and are not intended to be ornithologically correct. You can do the same thing to make this particular design match your wallpaper, even if your colors are different than the ones in this example.

The pen and ink with acrylic wash technique lends itself to this designer look beautifully. This is a very good project for beginners. Unless you get way out of the lines, it will look great, even with a minimum amount of shading.

I used 140 lb. cold pressed watercolor paper and black India ink with a Koh-I-Noor Rapidograph technical pen, tip size 0/.35.

Very lightly transfer only the main lines of the design, using graphite paper and a stylus. Pressing too hard will make grooves in your paper. Carbon paper will smear and leave a waxy film to which the watery paint will not adhere.

STEP: 2

Using the technical pen, lightly ink the basic drawing. Let this dry a minute, and begin inking in the shadow areas and details, referring frequently to the pattern on the previous page for placement. When inking is completed, allow the drawing to dry thoroughly. If the ink is not completely dry, it may blur when you begin to apply your acrylic washes.

Apply Redi-Mask on all areas which are to remain white on the design, such as on the beak, around the eye, on the stripes on the head, on the white tips of the feathers along the wings, and on the tiny white dots on the breast.

Prepare your watery puddles of paint in advance. I use a bubble watercolor tray when possible. If not available, a discarded egg carton will work fine. To prepare your paint, put approximately 1 teaspoonful of water into each cup on the tray before adding the acrylic paint. Add only a small (pea sized) amount of the following colors to each cup of water: CRM, YO, BS, and BU. Then mix a small amount of the following colors and add to cups of water:

Navy = 3 parts UB + 1 part BU
Dk. Blue-Green = Equal parts UB + HG
Tan = Equal parts YO + BU

Make sure you apply only the watery paint from these puddles when you begin doing your washes. Darker values of each color are created by layering washes. Allow the paper to dry between each application. For soft edges, immediately fade or wash out the edges of each wash as it applied unless you choose to have a sharp or "hard" edge. You should have a scrap piece of watercolor paper next to your design to test your stroke each time, before you apply to your painting.

STEP: 3

Start applying a wash of dark blue-green to the head, using your liner or small round brush. Quickly use a clean, wet round brush to fade this color down onto the cheek area so that the cheek remains a lighter color than the top of the head. It is always better to keep your washes very light and transparent. You can always add another wash later to deepen shadows and brighten colors. Darken the crest area, adding water as you work from back to front so that you will have a light highlight area on the front part of the crest, just above the eye.

Using the same color, begin washing in the tail feathers, leaving a white edge on the right side of each feather. When this is dry, deepen the shadow under the base of the tail with another wash of this color.

Begin washing in the dark blue-green along the back, keeping the color darkest along the top edge. Vary the color by adding a little navy here and there.

Wash the speculum on the back wing with the dark blue-green, leaving tips of the feathers white. Darken the top edge of each feather with a second wash of the same color.

Wash the top part of the back wing with navy. Darken the shadow area with a second wash of the same color and wash out the edge.

Wash the primary feathers and the speculum on the front wing with BU. Darken shadow areas with another wash of BU. Wash the secondary feathers with tan. With BS, apply a wash along the front edge of the wing and dabble loosely towards the back of the wing. Wash some of the BS along the neck and down onto the breast, being careful not to cover up white spots if you were not able to use Redi-Mask. Darken the bottom of the breast area with BU.

Wash some BU under the tail behind the legs, and on the tummy directly in front of the legs. The legs are washed in with YO, and shaded along the back with BU.

The eye and the red area on the bill are washed in with CRM. Do not wash out the edges. It will take two or three washes of CRM to make the bill nice and bright. Add a touch of YO between the bill and cheek. Leave a small area at the base of the bill white. Add a white highlight in the pupil with Redi-White.

STEP: 4

Apply additional washes to intensify color where needed, and to deepen shadow areas. When these washes are completely dry, erase Redi-Mask and touch up any inked areas that may need emphasis. Sign and mat.

I chose a navy mat to frame this duck, and I positioned the opening of the mat in a diamond shape. This idea also came from the wallpaper book.

You may elect to add a special designer touch around the opening of the mat as I have done. Here is a helpful way to space a repeat border design evenly. Using tracing paper positioned over the mat opening, place a motif at each end of the border. Place the third motif in the center of these two. Either measure the distance or fold the paper so that the end motifs are aligned, one on top of the other and get an exact center. Sketch in this center motif. Continue to divide each space between motifs in half, adding an additional motif each time, until they are appropriately spaced along the border. Do this for each side of the mat opening. Transfer your completed design to the mat border. If you are using a dark mat, use white graphite to transfer the design; for a light mat, use the charcoal. I used a liner brush and Redi-White to apply these lines around the opening of this mat board.

Add a frame with glass and you have a "designer" masterpiece!

Florals done using pen and ink with Acrylic washes are particularly beautiful. Often with florals, I intentionally allow the color to spill over, outside the ink, in areas for a looser effect.

Visit your local wallpaper store for a smorgasbord of designs and ideas to add that extra special touch to your decor!

FLOWER GARDEN

You don't need a green thumb to grow this beautiful garden of flowers. All you need is:

Ultramarine Blue (UB)   Burnt Umber (BU)
Indo Orange Red (IOR)   Acra Violet (AV)
Permanent Green Light (PGL) Yellow Ochre (YO)
Redi-White (RW)

(Pattern is actual size for 16x20 canvas)

Flowers are the actual size I used. You will need to add more and move flowers around to fit the size surface you select.

STEP: 1

PREMIX YOUR COLORS:
Light Peach = IOR + Redi-White
Purple = UB + AV
Maroon = AV + IOR

Wet your canvas thoroughly with water using your natural sponge. With your 2 inch blending brush, apply the light peach over your canvas, leaving a crescent area in the center blank. Darken the premixed peach one shade with a touch of additional IOR and BU. Brush this over and blend it into the peach at the bottom of the canvas only. This gives a slightly darker peach below your bouquet. Apply the premixed colors in the blank area. Notice color placement in the photograph above. The dark colors should overlap the peach about 1/2 inch to allow the colors to blend out smoothly.

STEP: 2

Feather out the edges of the dark colors quickly with a clean, two-inch blending brush while the paint is still wet. Move quickly around the design. Be careful not to overblend. You want to see individual colors of purple, maroon, and IOR burst forth with loose, fluffy edges. Indicate definite placement for the hyacinths by using your fan brush to hook onto the dark colors in the crescent and tapping upward. Add subtle accents of color if needed and final smoothing can be done with a fan brush also. Leave distinct patches of purple, IOR, and maroon within the crescent also.

Lightly load your fan brush with thinned maroon and purple. Add transparent leaves in, and outside the design. The leaves are usually created with two quick strokes going in opposite directions. Start at the outside of the leaf and pull toward the center. Do not overlap the strokes as it will create an "X" in the center of your leaf.

STEP: 3

Medium Yellow = YO + Redi-White
Leaf Green = PGL + BU

You may wish to dry your background and indicate the placement of a few prominent flowers within the design. A dry undercoating is very forgiving. It will allow you to wipe off undesirable wet strokes and leave the dry background intact.

The large daisies are applied with the #6 round brush. If the background is still wet, begin with Redi-White only. If dry, double load your brush with the purple and Redi-White. Start at the tip of each petal and stroke toward the center. Do not fill in the center. Leave a circular area unpainted in the center of each daisy to accommodate the stamen. To make a daisy turn in a particular direction, make the petals shorter on that side. For example if you wanted a daisy to turn up, you would have

shorter petals on the top side.

Apply the stamen with the round brush double loaded with BU and medium yellow. Hold the brush so that the BU is on the bottom side and the yellow is on top. Tap around lightly in the center of the flower until you have created a stamen of the appropriate size.

The hyacinths are created by grouping a lot of tiny little flowers and strokes in a cone shape. Begin at the top of the hyacinth with the "feathered out" color on your round brush. Apply one stroke at the top and gradually add more as you move down the cone. Double load your round with the hyacinth color and Redi-White. Paint very small flowers with 4 or 5 petals randomly over the cone shape. Occasionally add odd petals, as it is unlikely that you would see each petal on every flower within the hyacinths. Add a few more flowers and petals with Redi-White.

For the violets use your round brush double loaded with purple and Redi-White. Notice the placement of light and dark in the photograph above. Apply the color from the outside of the flower working in toward the center. The top petals are applied first, the side petals next, and the bottom large petal last. The bottom petal is actually two strokes with the purple touching, back to back. Add a tiny stamen with BU and medium yellow in the center of each violet.

Apply the shadow color for the baby's breath with your sponge using a light lavender mixture of Redi-White and purple. Highlight the tops of the baby's breath with your sponge using Redi-White. Cluster the stems underneath and the flowers become Queen Ann's Lace!

Add stems through out the composition with a double loaded liner brush using very thin leaf green and medium yellow. Study the finished product for each stem placement and shape.

STEP: 4

Light Blue = Ultramarine Blue + Redi-White
Light Orange = Indo Orange Red + Redi-White
Light Violet = Acra Violet + Redi-White

Tiny "filler" daisies are done in a variety of colors from your palette to include the ones mentioned above. They are applied with the round brush in the same manner as the large ones. The centers of the daisies are done with YO and BU.

After your flowers are dry, add ink like washes of color over anywhere you feel that you need a little extra contrast or shadow. Sometimes a sparkle of white over a dry wash is just what the doctor ordered to add depth to a flower. For example, sometimes I add shadows to the daisy petals, moving from the center toward the outer edges. Don't take the shadow color all the way to the end of the petals. Add the final petals with pure Redi-White to the flowers.

Add double loaded leaves with your round and angle brush, using leaf green and medium yellow.

Speckle the bottom and left side of your canvas with several dark and light colors from your painting using your fan brush or an old toothbrush.

Back away and take a look at the overall composition before you make changes. Add "fillers" or "do-fers" sparingly as it can easily become too busy and cluttered.

This technique could be used to match any color scheme you desire and could easily be enlarged to an over-the-sofa size or larger.

Sign, seal, and stop to smell the flowers along your way!

I hope you have had fun with the paintings in this series. Be sure to look for my other books and TV programs, "Wonderful World of Acrylics," "Acrylic Art is Fun" and "Acrylic Art is Fun II." They are packed full of interesting techniques you can achieve with acrylics.

NEW
PROJECT PACKS

BRENDA HARRIS

"Out Of The Shadows"
#1210

"Large Mouth Bass"
#1215

"The Home Place"
#1213

"Moonlighting"
#1214

"Coastal Lookout"
#1211

"A Day At The Beach"
#1212

These great NEW PROJECT PACKS provide DETAILED INSTRUCTION for ONE PAINTING. Each Packet includes a color photograph of completed painting and all necessary patterns required.

Note Cards

ARTIST CARDS
By **BRENDA HARRIS** TV Artist

24 Cards and Envelopes, 6 Each of 4 Designs

"You write your own greeting inside"

Original Art For Sale

ORIGINALS by BRENDA HARRIS are very affordable and are available direct to you from her studio. When writing send self-addressed, stamped envelope with your request or call:
B. Harris
P.O. Box 8761-B
Jacksonville, FL 32239
(904) 642-3076

70

Art-A-Peel

Art-A-Peel... peel and stick patterns. Each packet contains one sheet Saral graphite
paper and patterns in various sizes.

Art-A-Peel #8250; Canada Goose, Light House, Country Barn.
(from book 1 & 2)

Art-A-Peel #8252; Winter in New England, Bound for Glory, Wash Day.
(from book 3)

Art-A-Peel #8253; Free Lunch, Curing Time, Final Catch, Pigeon Point Lighthouse,
Rolling Meadows.

Seminar Calendar

Brenda travels extensively teaching approximately two hundred daily workshops per year. She may be scheduled
to come to your area soon. If not, you can be instrumental in organizing one. To receive a SEMINAR SCHEDULE
or obtain information call or send a legal size, self-addressed, stamped envelope with your request to:

b. Harris
P.O. Box 8761-B
Jacksonville, FL 32239

How would you like to vacation in Europe, Hawaii or possibly cruise the Caribbean and paint-along with Brenda
at the same time? Exotic workshop tours are available to you and your family at super saving fares. Send a self
addressed, stamped envelope along with your request to the above address.

Television Schedule

The Wonderful World of Acrylics and Acrylic Art is Fun I, II, and III are available to all Public Broadcasting
stations throughout the U.S., free of charge. Look in your yellow pages for the station in your area and call to see
the programs are aired, don't forget to say "Thanks". Program directors like to hear from and try to accomodate
viewers requests.

The Learning Channel, which is a selection on many cable networks also carries the above programs. Check your
guide for exact times.

Should you have a satelite dish, you can call Graphics Plus (1-800-328-6999) toll free, for time and frequency.

AS SEEN ON NATIONAL TELEVISION

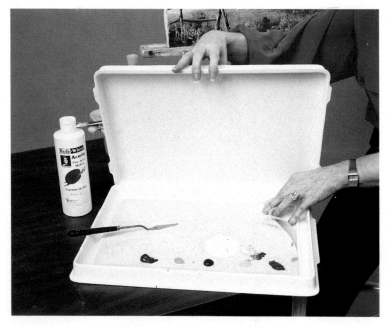

New Design

Redi-Wet™
ALL PURPOSE
PALETTE
• • System • •

REVOLUTIONIZES ACRYLIC PAINTING!
NO MORE DRYING OUT ON YOUR PALETTE.
DISPOSABLE PALETTE SHEETS!
INEXPENSIVE - ELIMINATES CLEAN UP.
EASY SNAP ON COVER

THE REDI-WET PALETTE SYSTEM is the most versatile palette for Artists. It works equally well for ACRYLICS, OILS AND WATERCOLOR. This easy-to-use palette keeps your paints from drying for days, even weeks.

FOR ACRYLICS: Palette comes with sponge, disposable palette paper and an easy snap on cover.

FOR OILS: Palette comes with disposable palette paper and an easy snap on cover.

Graphics Plus of Florida, Inc.

Producers of Educational Materials and Television Programs
400 N.E. Third Street • Delray Beach, Florida 33483 • (407) 278-6034
Toll Free Number 1-800-328-6999
Fax (407) 276-7644

72